Thuet

MARC THUET

MARC THUET

FRENCH FOOD MY WAY

VIKING
CANADA

VIKING CANADA

Published by the Penguin Group

Penguin Group (Canada), 90 Eglinton Avenue East, Suite 700,
Toronto, Ontario, Canada M4P 2Y3 (a division of Pearson Canada Inc.)

Penguin Group (USA) Inc., 375 Hudson Street, New York,
New York 10014, U.S.A.
Penguin Books Ltd, 80 Strand, London WC2R 0RL, England
Penguin Ireland, 25 St Stephen's Green, Dublin 2, Ireland
(a division of Penguin Books Ltd)
Penguin Group (Australia), 250 Camberwell Road, Camberwell,
Victoria 3124, Australia (a division of Pearson Australia Group Pty Ltd)
Penguin Books India Pvt Ltd, 11 Community Centre, Panchsheel Park,
New Delhi – 110 017, India
Penguin Group (NZ), 67 Apollo Drive, Rosedale, North Shore 0745, Auckland,
New Zealand (a division of Pearson New Zealand Ltd)
Penguin Books (South Africa) (Pty) Ltd, 24 Sturdee Avenue, Rosebank,
Johannesburg 2196, South Africa

Penguin Books Ltd, Registered Offices: 80 Strand, London WC2R 0RL, England

First published 2010

1 2 3 4 5 6 7 8 9 10

Manufactured in the U.S.A.

Cover and interior design: Mary Opper
Photography: Paula Wilson

LIBRARY AND ARCHIVES CANADA CATALOGUING IN PUBLICATION

Thuet, Marc
French food my way / Marc Thuet.

ISBN 978-0-670-06454-0

1. Cookery, French. I. Title.

TX719.T475 2010   641.5944   C2010-901984-9

Visit the Penguin Group (Canada) website at www.penguin.ca

Special and corporate bulk purchase rates available;
please see www.penguin.ca/corporatesales
or call 1-800-810-3104, ext. 2477 or 2474

To all those who've touched my life and passed on,
sharing with me an appreciation for all things epicurean

In memory of our dear friend Jocelyn Juriansz (1976–2005),
a portion of the royalties from this book will be donated to the
Jocelyn Juriansz Memorial Fund (jocelynjuriansz.com)
to help support women and children from neglected homes

CONTENTS

Take away infancy and early childhood—and some extracurricular activities that came later on—and my life has been pretty much about nothing but food and cooking. I grew up on a farm in Blodelsheim, in Alsace. The local bakery was called Boulangerie Thuet, named for my uncle Marcel. My other uncle, Pierro, was the chef and owner of a popular local game restaurant called Chez Pierre (named for an earlier Pierre—there have been chefs in the family for generations).

According to family legend, I had my first bath in the kitchen sink at the restaurant between services. Such was the devotion to the family business. By primary school I was spending more time harvesting and peeling white asparagus than doing my homework. Later, as a reward, I helped clean the kitchen at Chez Pierre and took care of odd jobs like skinning hare and plucking wild duck. At thirteen, I did my first catering—a communion, for about eighty people. It wasn't much—all I had to do was reheat the dishes, finish the sauces, and put it all on a plate—but I remember it well because it was my first time, and because when I was done, I thought to myself, "I'd really love to do this for the rest of my life."

So I learned the ropes at Chez Pierre, predominantly by way of hunting with my uncle, because that was one of his jobs: go out there, shoot, kill, and put it on the menu. The relationship with food is a little different in Europe—especially in Alsace. That's where I stayed when I left my uncle's restaurant, moving on to Lycée

Hôtelier de Strasbourg and then to some of the local Michelin-starred restaurants. After doing the rounds at some of the best kitchens in France, I headed for London to learn something new—one of my employers knew Anton Mosimann, who got me a job at the Dorchester in 1982.

That's where my cooking grew up. The dishes Chef Mosimann turned out of those kitchens were incredible. He was a great mentor to all of us who worked for him then, and to so many others. I still can hardly believe it when I think about the chefs who used to come to eat his food—our food—at the Dorchester in those days. Chefs who had two or three Michelin stars back then, when it was so hard to get just one. Chef Jacques Maximin used to come, and Chef Roger Vergé, and my hero, Chef Eckart Witzigmann, who had the three-starred Aubergine in Munich and published cookbooks twenty-five years ago with recipes that still look modern today. He knew how to party, too.

Chef Mosimann had a gift for re-creating old recipes with a fresh, original outlook. He revolutionized English food. He also had this incredible sense of season, and he tried to teach it to all his young chefs. Essentially, he lined us up against the wall in his kitchen every Monday morning and quizzed us: "What's coming out this week? What are we looking forward to next week?" It changed my view, made my focus a lot stronger, and paved the way for my later culinary adventures. Since London, I've never looked back—that's why this book is divided into recipes for spring, summer, fall, and winter. It's the only way to cook.

Chef Mosimann and I hit it off, which would be a bit of a surprise if you knew me and tried to imagine me having a deep bond with a man so proper and formal, driving around in his vintage Rolls-Royce. Anton was also responsible for my arriving in Toronto. When he was a young chef—just a teenager—he came to Canada for the opportunities at Expo 67 and ended up working at the Queen Elizabeth Hotel in Montreal, where he became sous-chef under a fellow Swiss, Chef Albert Schnell. Anton looked at Schnell the way I look at Chef Mosimann, as a mentor and an educator, and when I told him that I wanted to go to the States, he insisted I go first to Montreal to work for Chef Schnell.

In the meantime, Chef Schnell had moved on, to the Toronto Hilton, so that's where I went. He is the other great influence on this book—before him, all the European chefs who ran the great hotel kitchens were lazy snobs about where their food and ingredients came from. They didn't care about costs because they worked for big chains and didn't have to, so whatever they wanted, they ordered to be flown in from France. Chef Schnell was the first to look around and realize how great Canadian produce was. Without him, there wouldn't be a recipe in this book for that French classic quenelles de brochet sauce Nantua (crayfish) made with Ontario Lake pickerel and Nova Scotia lobster. It would instead be made here in Canada with a French pike (brochet) and North Sea lobster sauce. Things have changed so much since Chef Schnell took the first steps to dignify Canadian producers that it's hard to remember how big a deal that was when it first happened.

The other message I've tried to get across in this book is the importance of passion. Cooking is the biggest passion of my life, and every time I talk to people about their work I end up thinking how lucky I am, because I love what I do, and I go to sleep at night excited about getting back to work the next day. I think that's one of the reasons I experiment so much in my kitchen, because the only thing in life that scares me is the thought that cooking could get boring one day.

It should never be boring for you. I encourage you to have fun in your kitchen. Play music, like we do in our kitchen at work, whether it's classical or Jay-Z. Have a drink, like I used to (okay, sometimes I had two). Have friends over, let them help, have a blast. Most important, don't worry so much about following these recipes to the letter, or decide you can't make something just because you don't have one of the ingredients. Think of these recipes as guides, just like the pamphlet you got at driving school. You don't still drive the way it said you were supposed to, do you? And that's okay, as long as you avoid having accidents.

In the kitchen, as on the road, confidence comes with practice and experience. You'll also do better if you think about what's in season and buy your ingredients from the best artisanal suppliers you can find. Start with the recipes you're comfortable you can pull off, then try the harder ones when you feel you can handle them. In this book, you'll find the easier recipes are those for earlier in the day, and the harder ones for dinner. You can make whatever changes you like with all of them—as long as they make sense. You want to use buffalo instead of beef, or guinea hen instead of chicken? Go for it. It might be good! It might even be better than what I put down on the page.

Cuisinement votre,
Marc Thuet

For me the most basic expression of spring cooking is lamb. One reason is that if you grew up Catholic, like me, the first festive meal of the season is Easter, and for that, lamb is the traditional main event. The other reason—and this is worth explaining when you're used to seeing "spring lamb" stamped on frozen racks of New Zealand mutton in January—is that spring and lamb are simply supposed to go together, and when they do, it means something special.

In France, the first lamb of spring is a delicacy we call *agnelet*, or milk lamb. Yes, we whack them before they're weaned, at age thirty to forty days, when they weigh 10 kilos at the most. We do this for two good reasons. In a place like Roquefort, the mother's milk is saved for cheese. And this baby lamb has the most tender, sweet flesh you can imagine. It's not even pink yet—it has a light bluish tinge. The eye of the rack is the size of your thumbnail. Roasted lightly and served with wild leeks, it's my favourite spring meal.

That brings me to the other fantastic thing about spring—foraging. People think of me as a hunter, but I like looking around in the woods for the first wild crops of the season just as much. After the long winter, and its rich reductions and sauces, nothing can beat the bright colours and delicate flavours of fiddleheads, wild leeks, and morels—my favourite fungus, after the truffle.

I grew up on a farm in Alsace, and there spring brought the most treasured crop—white asparagus. Then there are all those fresh, delicate herbs and greens, like sorrel, the perfect flavour match for salmon, taken on its first spring run. Every spring I think to myself, "This is the best time of year to cook." Then it's summer and I think the same thing all over again.

BREAKFAST

Pancakes with Mango Coulis   6

Maple-Crusted Granola with Sheep's Milk Yogurt and Strawberries   7

Poached Duck Eggs with Maple-Glazed Peameal Bacon and Rösti Potatoes   8

LUNCH APPETIZER

Wild Leek and Fingerling Potato Soup with Smoked B.C. Salmon   11

Crispy Ricotta-Stuffed Zucchini Blossoms with Green Onion Purée   12

LUNCH SANDWICH

Avocado, Lobster, Dungeness Crab, and Whitefish Caviar Sandwich   16

LUNCH MAIN COURSE

Grilled Sourdough Lamb Sandwich with Green Asparagus and Goat Cheese   17

Braised Lamb Shanks with Artichoke Barigoule   20

Pappardelle with Braised Rabbit and Bluefoot Mushrooms in a Wild Chervil Essence   23

Poached Pickerel with Ragoût of Clams, Mussels, Escargots, and Chorizo Sausage   27

Quenelles of Northern Lake Pike with Lobster Sauce   28

Lobster Lasagnette   31

DINNER APPETIZER

Rabbit Loin Salad with White Asparagus and Pineapple Butter   32

Potage of Frogs' Legs with Riesling and Morels   34

Lamb Tartare with Mâche Salad, Rondoudou Ashed Goat Cheese, and Poached Rhubarb   36

Pancakes with Mango Coulis

My favourite breakfast to make for my children on Sunday mornings.

SERVES 4

Mango coulis (see p. 227)
1²/₃ cups (400 mL) all-purpose flour
¼ cup (50 mL) sugar
2 tbsp (30 mL) baking powder
1 tsp (5 mL) salt
²/₃ cup (150 mL) whole milk
²/₃ cup (150 mL) buttermilk
½ cup (125 mL) butter, melted
2 eggs
2 tbsp (30 mL) butter, for frying
½ cup (125 mL) maple sugar
Finely chopped mango, maple syrup,
    and fresh mint leaves to garnish

Preheat the oven to 350°F (180°C).

Prepare the coulis in a small saucepan and set aside. Sift the flour, sugar, baking powder, and salt into a large mixing bowl.

Whisk the whole milk, buttermilk, melted butter, and eggs in a separate bowl. Pour over the dry ingredients, stirring continuously. Set the batter aside to rise for 10 minutes.

Warm a medium-sized cast-iron or oven-safe nonstick pan and add 2 tbsp (30 mL) butter (or less, as required). Caramelize the butter slightly until brown around the edges. Add ¼ cup (50 mL) of the pancake batter, or enough to coat your pan with a thick layer.

Move the pan to the oven and cook for about 5 minutes until the bottom is golden brown. Flip the pancake and bake 5 minutes longer. Cool and cut out 2 or 3 pancakes using a medium-sized (about 2-inch) cookie cutter. Repeat these steps using the rest of the batter.

Spoon 1 tbsp (15 mL) of the mango coulis onto each serving plate. Dip one side of each pancake lightly in the leftover syrup in the saucepan, taking care not to touch the fruit. Gently press in maple sugar until lightly coated. Place the pancakes on top of the coulis, sugar-coated side facing up. Top with finely chopped mango and drizzle with remaining mango coulis and maple syrup. Garnish with mint leaves.

NOTE: This recipe makes small portions, so you may double recipe if you wish. Maple sugar is available from most maple syrup producers and retailers.

Maple-Crusted Granola with Sheep's Milk Yogurt and Strawberries

We make our own yogurt with sheep's milk from Misty Ridge Farms in eastern Ontario. Love it.

SERVES 4

STRAWBERRY COULIS
1½ cups (375 mL) whole strawberries
⅓ cup (75 mL) white sugar

MAPLE-CRUSTED GRANOLA WITH YOGURT
2 cups (500 mL) maple syrup
2 cups (500 mL) old-fashioned brown sugar
2 cups (500 mL) rolled oats
1 cup (250 mL) whole almonds
1 cup (250 mL) whole hazelnuts
1 cup (250 mL) chopped walnuts
1 cup (250 mL) chopped pecans
½ cup (125 mL) sunflower seeds
½ cup (125 mL) pumpkin seeds

½ cup (125 mL) dark flaxseed
½ cup (125 mL) golden flaxseed
1 cup (250 mL) golden raisins
1 cup (250 mL) chopped dried figs
1 cup (250 mL) chopped dried apricots
½ cup (125 mL) dried cranberries
4 cups (1 L) sheep's milk yogurt
Fresh mint leaves to garnish

Preheat the oven to 375°F (190°C).

To prepare the coulis, combine the strawberries and sugar in a saucepan. Simmer over low heat until the sugar is completely melted. Set aside.

Warm the maple syrup and brown sugar in a small saucepan. Simmer until the sugar has completely dissolved.

Spread the oats on one baking tray; the almonds, hazelnuts, walnuts, and pecans on another; and the sunflower seeds, pumpkin seeds, and flaxseed on a third tray.

Dry roast for 7 to 10 minutes until golden brown, removing the nuts first, then the seeds, and finally the oats.

Toss the roasted nuts, seeds, and oats with the raisins, figs, apricots, cranberries, and sugar solution, stirring until well coated. Spread on a baking tray and bake for 7 minutes, taking care not to burn the mixture. (If in doubt, it's better to bake the granola for less time. It will harden as it cools.)

Remove from the oven and cool for several hours, preferably overnight. The mixture should break easily in your hands.

Spoon the granola into 4 martini glasses. Top each with 2 tbsp (30 mL) yogurt and 1 tbsp (15 mL) coulis, adding additional layers as desired. Garnish with fresh mint leaves.

NOTE: You may find it helpful to prepare the granola the night before serving. Goat's milk or any thick, quality yogurt can be used if sheep's milk yogurt is not readily available.

Poached Duck Eggs with Maple-Glazed Peameal Bacon and Rösti Potatoes

I first tasted this bacon when I came to Canada and thought it was incredibly flavourful. Today, I make my own at the restaurant, using the proper yellow pea flour instead of cornmeal.

SERVES 4

12 medium-sized potatoes
½ cup (125 mL) butter
8 rashers (slices) peameal bacon
½ cup (125 mL) maple syrup
4 duck eggs (or chicken eggs)
⅓ cup (75 mL) white vinegar

Preheat the oven to 325°F (160°C).

Wash and peel the potatoes, then grate using a mandoline or the largest holes on your grater. Generously coat a cast-iron or oven-safe nonstick pan with canola oil and warm over medium heat. Add the potato and flatten with the blunt side of a large knife. Top with a generous knob of butter, about ¼ cup (50 mL). Cook for 3 minutes or until the sides turn golden brown. Transfer the pan to the oven and bake for 25 minutes until golden brown all over and crispy on the sides.

Warm the remaining ¼ cup (50 mL) butter in a medium-sized cast-iron or nonstick pan. Fry the peameal bacon in the butter over medium heat until both sides are slightly brown. Remove from the pan and dip both sides of the bacon in maple syrup. Return the bacon to the pan for approximately 2 minutes, but *do not turn on the heat.*

Meanwhile, poach the eggs in a medium saucepan of water and the white vinegar until the yolk is soft and runny.

Top each piece of the rösti potato with 2 slices of bacon and balance a poached duck egg on top.

NOTE: The size of the pan for the rösti will depend on what you have available. You'll need about 3 potatoes per serving. You may want to make one large rösti and cut it into 4 pieces or cook each rösti separately in 4 small pans.

One of the biggest adventures for my kitchen brigade is picking the first wild leeks of spring in rural Ontario. But once the soup is simmering, the early morning wakeup call is instantly forgotten.

SERVES 4

3 tbsp (45 mL) butter
4 cups (1 L) cleaned and chopped wild leeks (leaves and bulbs)
3 cups (750 mL) peeled and diced fingerling potatoes
6 cups (1.5 L) chicken stock (see p. 215)
Dash salt
Dash pepper
1 cup (250 mL) whipping cream
1 cup (250 mL) whipped cream
4 slices smoked wild B.C. salmon

In a rondeau or large sauté pan, melt 2 tbsp (30 mL) of the butter. Add 3 cups (750 mL) of the wild leeks; sauté for a few minutes.

Stir in the potatoes and chicken stock and bring to a simmer. Season with salt and pepper. Simmer until the potatoes are tender. Add the whipping cream and the remaining wild leeks. Bring back to a simmer for another 5 minutes.

Purée the soup in a blender until creamy. Pour the soup through a chinois (a cone-shaped, fine mesh sieve) back into the rondeau. Just before serving, bring the soup to a low simmer. With a hand blender whisk in the remaining butter and whipped cream until frothy.

Arrange the smoked salmon in a rosette in the middle of 4 warm soup bowls. Pour the hot, frothy soup around the smoked salmon and not over the top.

We make a point of rising even earlier to hit the market during zucchini flower season. If we're a little late, these precious "roses" will have happily found their way into someone else's kitchen.

SERVES 4

GREEN ONION PURÉE
¾ cup (175 mL) sliced green onion
¼ cup (50 mL) butter
⅓ cup (75 mL) chicken stock
   (see p. 215)
Salt and pepper to taste

ZUCCHINI BLOSSOMS
2 cups (500 mL) ricotta cheese
1 tbsp (15 mL) finely chopped chives
1 tbsp (15 mL) finely chopped shallots
Salt and pepper to taste
8 zucchini blossoms
4 eggs
½ cup (125 mL) ice water
1 cup (250 mL) all-purpose flour
2 tsp (10 mL) salt
2 tsp (10 mL) cornstarch
1 tsp (5 mL) sugar
Peanut oil for deep-frying
½ cup (125 mL) olive oil
½ cup (125 mL) green oil (see p. 226)
½ cup (125 mL) balsamic
   vinegar glaze (see p. 93)
Fresh herbs and edible flowers
   to garnish

To make the green onion purée, sweat the green onions in the butter over low heat, ensuring they retain their colour. Remove from heat and transfer to a food processor. Add the chicken stock, salt, and pepper. Emulsify to a thick paste.

For the zucchini blossoms, combine the ricotta, chives, and shallots; season with salt and pepper. Remove the stamens or pistils from the zucchini blossoms. Carefully stuff each flower with the mixture, using a piping bag if available. Refrigerate overnight.

The following day, prepare the zucchini batter by whisking together the eggs and water. Add the flour, salt, cornstarch, and sugar, whisking until thick but still pourable.

Dip each stuffed zucchini blossom gently in the batter, ensuring that it's fully coated. Heat the peanut oil in a deep, heavy-bottomed pot to 375°F (190°C). Fry the zucchini blossoms until golden brown, 3 to 4 minutes.

Cut the stalks and halve each blossom lengthwise. Serve 1½ blossoms per person. Drizzle with the olive oil, green oil, and balsamic vinegar reduction. Serve with the green onion purée and garnish with fresh herbs and edible flowers.

Avocado, Lobster, Dungeness Crab, and Whitefish Caviar Sandwich

The MVP of all sandwiches sold at our Petite Thuet bakeries. We use Thuet Bakery pretzel buns, but savoury bread or milk buns also work well. Please don't use a baguette.

SERVES 4

2 1-lb (500 g) live lobsters
8 cups (2 L) court bouillon (see p. 224)
1½-lb (750 g) Dungeness crab
Avocado oil mayonnaise (see p. 226)
2 tsp (10 mL) finely chopped chives
1 tsp (5 mL) finely chopped green onion
Salt and pepper to taste
4 savoury buns
1 avocado
4 tsp (20 mL) whitefish caviar
Arugula leaves to garnish

Boil the lobsters in court bouillon for about 5 minutes; remove lobsters and cool in a bowl of iced water. Pick the meat from the shell and set aside. Simmer the crab in the court bouillon for 7 minutes (depending on the size—aim for 5 minutes per pound); remove and cool in a bowl of iced water. Take the meat from the shell and mix with 2 tbsp (30 mL) of the avocado oil mayonnaise, the chives, the green onion, and salt and pepper to taste.

Cut the buns in half lengthwise and spread the remaining avocado mayonnaise on both sides. Peel, quarter, and slice the avocado. Spread a generous amount of the crab mixture on one side of each bun and top with a quarter of the avocado per sandwich. Place a quarter of the lobster meat on each sandwich and sprinkle with 1 tsp (5 mL) whitefish caviar. Scatter with arugula leaves, close, and serve.

Grilled Sourdough Lamb Sandwich with Green Asparagus and Goat Cheese

When I worked in the south of France, I used to enjoy this sandwich on the patio in Cassis overlooking the Mediterranean.

SERVES 4

LEG OF LAMB

1 leg of lamb, deboned, as much fat
    and silverskin removed as possible
4 whole garlic cloves
Butter and oil for searing
Salt and pepper to taste
1 sprig rosemary
1 sprig thyme

ASPARAGUS AND GRILLED SOURDOUGH

4 slices sourdough bread
2 tbsp (30 mL) olive oil
1 garlic clove, crushed
20 pieces asparagus
Salt to taste
5 oz (150 g) ashed goat cheese
4 quail eggs, fried
4 tsp (20 mL) coriander aïoli (see p. 224)
Organic coriander shoots to garnish

Preheat the oven to 500°F (260°C).

To prepare the lamb, pierce and stuff with the garlic cloves. Tie with string, season, and sear in butter and olive oil in a small cast-iron or oven-safe nonstick pan over high heat. Sear on all sides until slightly brown around the edges, 3 to 4 minutes in total.

Remove the pan from the heat and tuck the rosemary and thyme sprigs under the string. Place in the oven to roast for 35 minutes.

Brush the bread with some of the olive oil and the garlic, and grill or pan-fry over medium heat until golden brown. Brush the asparagus with the remaining olive oil, season with salt, and grill until al dente.

On each sourdough slice, arrange 3 to 5 slices of the lamb, 3 slices of goat cheese, 5 pieces of asparagus, and a fried quail egg. Top with 1 tsp (5 mL) coriander aïoli and garnish with coriander shoots.

Braised Lamb Shanks with Artichoke Barigoule

The preparation of this dish ignites what I like to call "lamb foreplay." The earthy aroma of the meat fills not only the kitchen but the entire house. Once you plate it, you'll understand the value of the three-hour courtship.

SERVES 4

BRAISED LAMB SHANKS

4 lamb shanks

Salt and pepper to taste

½ cup (125 mL) butter

½ cup (125 mL) olive oil

2 carrots, cut into ¼-inch (5 mm) rounds

1 onion, chopped

½ celery stalk, chopped

5 tomatoes, cubed

4 garlic cloves, crushed

1 tsp (5 mL) chopped fresh rosemary

1 tsp (5 mL) chopped fresh thyme

1 6-oz (170 g) can tomato paste

4 cups (1 L) lamb jus (see p. 219)

BRAISED ARTICHOKE BARIGOULE WITH TOMATO CONCASSÉ

16 artichokes

1 onion, chopped

2 garlic cloves, minced

½ cup (125 mL) diced speck (or smoked or cooked ham)

2 tbsp (30 mL) grapeseed oil

1 cup (250 mL) white wine

1 cup (250 mL) water

4 whole tomatoes

2 tbsp (30 mL) olive oil

2 tsp (10 mL) chopped fresh basil

Oven-roasted cherry tomatoes (yellow and red) and chopped fresh basil to garnish

Preheat the oven to 350°F (180°C).

Season the lamb shanks. Heat the butter and olive oil in a large cast-iron pan over high heat. Sear the lamb on all sides until the edges are golden brown; set aside.

In a rondeau or sauté pan, sauté the carrots, onion, and celery until browned. Add the cubed tomatoes, garlic, rosemary, and thyme; sauté for another 5 minutes, being careful not to burn the vegetables. Stir in the tomato paste, mixing well. Add the lamb stock and bring to a boil.

Arrange the lamb shanks in a roasting pan. Pour in the stock and vegetable mixture, cover, and braise in the oven for 90 minutes.

Meanwhile, to make the artichoke barigoule, sauté the artichokes, onion, garlic, and speck in grapeseed oil until browned. Pour in the white wine. Simmer and reduce by half, until the alcohol has cooked off. Add the cup of water, or as much as needed to cover. Simmer gently for 20 minutes until the artichokes are tender. Remove the artichokes, discarding the braising liquid. Cool and peel the outer layers to expose the artichoke hearts.

To prepare the tomato concassé, make a small cross or incision in the base of each tomato with a sharp knife. Plunge the tomatoes into a saucepan of boiling water for about 1 minute; remove and cool in a bowl of ice water. Peel and cut lengthwise into strips. Briefly sauté with the artichoke hearts in olive oil until heated. Sprinkle with fresh basil.

Divide the artichokes and tomato concassé evenly among 4 serving plates, topping with a braised lamb shank. Garnish with oven-roasted cherry tomatoes and extra chopped basil.

NOTE: To oven-dry the tomatoes, place sliced cherry tomatoes in a roasting pan in a single layer. Drizzle generously with olive oil and season with salt and pepper to taste. Sprinkle with chopped fresh thyme and basil. Roast in a 150°F (65°C) oven for 9 hours.

Pappardelle with Braised Rabbit and Bluefoot Mushrooms in a Wild Chervil Essence

If I were Italian, this dish would forever be my staple. Pasta, rabbit, and mushrooms. What more could a man want?

SERVES 4

BRAISED RABBIT
1 2½- to 3-lb (1.25 kg to 1.5 kg) whole rabbit
4 cups (1 L) white wine (preferably
    Sauvignon Blanc)
1 medium carrot, peeled and chopped
1 leek, cleaned and chopped (white part only)
1 medium onion, chopped
8 garlic cloves, peeled
20 black peppercorns
4 juniper berries
1 bay leaf
1 sprig thyme
1 sprig rosemary
Salt and pepper to taste
3 tbsp (45 mL) canola oil
4 Roma tomatoes, chopped
4 cups (1 L) dark chicken stock (see p. 216)

MUSHROOMS
2 tbsp (30 mL) grapeseed oil
8 oz (225 g) bluefoot, king oyster,
    or shiitake mushrooms
1 tbsp (15 mL) chopped shallots
Salt and pepper
4 oz (120 g) speck (or lightly smoked bacon)
4 tbsp (60 mL) butter

PAPPARDELLE
1 lb (500 g) pappardelle
2 tbsp (30 mL) olive oil
1 tbsp (15 mL) chopped fresh chervil
    (preferably wild)
4 sprigs chervil to garnish

Preheat the oven to 350°F (180°C).

Cut up the rabbit into front and hind legs and saddle. Marinate in the white wine, carrots, leeks, onion, garlic, peppercorns, juniper berries, bay leaf, thyme, and rosemary for 24 hours.

Remove the rabbit pieces from the marinade. Pour the marinade through a chinois (sieve) and set aside. Place the vegetables and spices remaining in the chinois in cheesecloth and tie with butcher's string to form a small bag.

Season the rabbit with salt and pepper. Heat the canola oil in a skillet and sauté until golden brown. Remove the rabbit to a braising pan. In the same skillet, sauté the chopped tomatoes for a few minutes until soft, being careful not to burn them.

Deglaze the pan with the marinating liquid. Add the dark chicken stock, bring to a simmer, and pour the liquid over the rabbit pieces, making sure they're covered. Add the spice and vegetable bag to the braising pan, cover with a lid, and place in the preheated oven. Braise until the meat begins to pull away from the bone, 1½ to 2 hours.

Remove the pan from oven and set aside until the rabbit is cool enough to handle. Pull the meat from the bones and set aside. Strain the braising liquid and skim off any fat. Return the liquid to the pan and reduce by half.

Heat the grapeseed oil in a large cast-iron pan. Sauté the mushrooms with the shallots; season with salt and pepper. Add the mushrooms and shallots, smoked pork belly, and rabbit meat to the braising liquid, bringing to a simmer. Whisk in the butter and slowly simmer for a few minutes until the sauce begins to thicken slightly.

Bring a large pot of salted water to a boil. Cook the pappardelle until al dente; drain and toss with the olive oil. Add the pappardelle to the braised rabbit; season with salt and pepper. Just before serving, sprinkle with chopped chervil.

Divide the pasta among 4 warm pasta bowls and garnish each with a sprig of chervil.

Poached Pickerel with Ragoût of Clams, Mussels, Escargots, and Chorizo Sausage

Georgian Bay pickerel is an underrated fish in Canada. The pickerel garners much more respect in Europe, where it's prized for its white, toothsome flesh. Every time I make this dish I reflect on how lucky we are to live near the Great Lakes and get the catch of the day.

SERVES 4

4 shallots, finely chopped
2 tsp (10 mL) butter
20 mussels
4 cups (1 L) white wine
20 clams
1 cup (250 mL) fish stock (see p. 216)
4 pieces pickerel, approx. 5 oz (150 g) each

1 tsp (5 mL) chopped fresh tarragon
1 tsp (5 mL) chopped fresh basil
12 escargots, washed
1½ oz (45 g) cured chorizo, thinly sliced
1 tsp (5 mL) lemon juice
Salt and pepper to taste
4 sprigs tarragon to garnish

In a large saucepan, sauté half the shallots in 1 tsp (5 mL) of the butter over medium-high heat until translucent. Add the mussels and 2 cups (500 mL) of the white wine, or enough to cover. Cook until the mussels open, about 2 minutes.

In a separate pan, sauté the remaining butter and shallots. Add the clams and the remaining wine. Cook until the clams open, about 5 minutes.

Remove the mussels and clams from the liquid and set aside. When cool, remove from their shells, keeping the shells for garnish. Strain the remaining liquids through cheesecloth or a fine sieve and combine. Reduce by half and stir in the fish stock. Bring back to a boil, lower the heat, and simmer gently.

Submerge the pickerel in the sauce and poach for about 3 minutes. Remove the fish with a slotted spoon and place on 4 prewarmed serving plates. Stir the tarragon and basil into the sauce and simmer until reduced by half, about 10 minutes.

Just before serving, add the mussels, clams, escargots, and sliced chorizo to the sauce and heat for about 30 seconds. Remove from the sauce and divide among the plates, arranging around the pickerel. Garnish each plate with 1 or 2 shells.

Stir the lemon juice into the sauce and season to taste. Divide the liquid equally among the dishes and garnish with tarragon sprigs. Serve with baby carrots and fresh garden peas.

Quenelles of Northern Lake Pike with Lobster Sauce

In Alsace, the pike is called the "king of the river." When I was a kid, my grandmother cooked it over her wood stove on special occasions. The lobster sauce is my Canadian twist on this very special dish.

SERVES 4

PANADE
1 cup (250 mL) milk
2 tbsp (30 mL) butter
2 cups (500 mL) all-purpose flour
1 egg

FISH MOUSSE
1 lb (500 g) pickerel fillet
3¾ cups (925 mL) melted butter
3 eggs
3 egg whites
3½ cups (875 mL) whipping cream
Salt, pepper, and nutmeg to taste

LOBSTER SAUCE
½ cup (125 mL) butter
1 cup (250 mL) all-purpose flour
2½ cups (625 mL) lobster stock (see p. 220)
2¼ cups (550 mL) whipping cream

Preheat the oven to 350°F (180°C).

Prepare the panade by combining the milk and butter in a saucepan and bringing to a boil. Slowly whisk in the flour, beating until smooth. Remove from the heat and beat in the egg. Return to the heat and stir energetically with a wooden spoon until the mixture comes away from the sides and the base of the pan. Set aside to cool.

To make the mousse, pound the raw fillets and pass through a coarse sieve. Transfer to a mixing bowl and gradually stir in the panade. Slowly beat in the melted butter and then the eggs, one at a time. In a separate bowl, beat the egg whites until stiff, then fold, with the cream, into the mousse. Season to taste with salt, pepper, and nutmeg. Set aside to cool in the fridge.

For the sauce, melt the butter gently over low heat and slowly stir in the flour, mixing until smooth. Gradually stir in the lobster stock and the cream; continue cooking and stirring for a further 10 minutes. Remove from the heat and transfer the warm mixture to a double boiler.

Thirty-five minutes before serving, divide the chilled panade into 8 equal parts. Roll each part into a sausage-shaped piece on a lightly floured board. Bring 8 cups (2 litres) of salted water to a gentle simmer. Add the dumplings and poach for 12 minutes.

Meanwhile, pour the lobster sauce into a warm, oven-proof dish. Remove the dumplings from the water with a slotted spoon and arrange them in the sauce. Bake for 15 minutes and serve with the fish mousse.

Lobster Lasagne

Lobster, fresh pasta. Simple and sexy. This elegant dish is always a pleaser.

SERVES 4

LOBSTER
6 shallots, coarsely chopped
1 bouquet soft herbs (tarragon, parsley, chervil, and dill)
1 tsp (5 mL) salt
2 1½-lb (750 g) live lobsters

LOBSTER SAUCE
1 tbsp (15 mL) olive oil
1 tbsp (15 mL) butter
4 large shallots, roughly chopped
1 bunch parsley, chopped
½ leek, roughly chopped
3½ oz (100 g) plum tomatoes, chopped
6 cups (1.5 L) fish stock (see p. 216)
¾ cup (175 mL) whipping cream
Salt and pepper to taste
1 bunch chives, snipped

PASTA
8 2½- by 5-inch (6 by 12 cm) fresh pasta sheets
Salt and pepper to taste
1 tsp (5 mL) olive oil

Preheat the oven to 300°F (150°C).

To prepare the lobsters, fill a large saucepan with water. Add the shallots, soft herb bouquet, and salt and bring to a boil. Lower in the lobsters, bring back to a boil, and cook for 6 minutes. Carefully remove the lobsters and immediately plunge into ice water. When the lobsters have cooled, twist off the large claws and the body and head sections from the tail. Using a pair of sturdy scissors, carefully snip along the length of the tail shell and ease the meat from the shell. Gently break the shells of the claws and extract the meat. Set all the meat aside, retaining the shells (with the exception of the claws) for the lobster sauce.

To make the lobster sauce, arrange the lobster shells in a roasting pan and roast in the preheated oven for approximately 20 minutes to allow the shells to dry out. Meanwhile, heat the oil and butter in a saucepan and sweat the shallots, parsley, and leeks. Add the roasted lobster shells, the tomatoes, and enough of the fish stock to cover. Bring to a slow boil, then reduce the heat and simmer gently for an hour.

Remove the saucepan from the heat and transfer the contents to a food processor, blending until smooth. Pass the mixture through a fine sieve into a clean saucepan. Bring to a simmer over medium heat and reduce by about half. Whisk in the cream and season to taste with salt (if necessary) and freshly ground black pepper. Set aside.

Divide the lobster meat into 8 portions on a greased baking tray, giving each a little claw meat as well as tail meat. Cover each portion with 3 tbsp (45 mL) of the lobster sauce; cover the baking tray with plastic wrap. Place in the oven to warm through while you cook the pasta. Stir the chives into the remaining lobster sauce and set aside.

Drop the pasta sheets into a pan of gently boiling salted water. Cook for about 3 minutes, then carefully remove using a slotted spoon. Season with salt and pepper and splash with the olive oil.

On 4 prewarmed serving plates, lay a sheet of pasta and top with a portion of lobster. Cover with another pasta sheet and a second portion of the lobster. Spoon over the remainder of the lobster sauce. Serve with seasonal vegetables.

Rabbit Loin Salad with White Asparagus and Pineapple Butter

To me, rabbit meat is like a vintage dress to a couturier. It may be forgotten and a bit dusty, but once you try it, you'll appreciate its original glory and beauty.

SERVES 4

PINEAPPLE BUTTER
1 pineapple
1 tbsp (15 mL) butter

WHITE ASPARAGUS
20 pieces white asparagus
1 tbsp (15 mL) butter
1 tbsp (15 mL) salt
1 tsp (5 mL) sugar

RABBIT LOIN
1 loin of rabbit, cut in 4 sections
    or pieces
1 tsp (5 mL) chopped fresh thyme
1 tsp (5 mL) chopped fresh tarragon
1 tsp (5 mL) chopped fresh rosemary
1 tsp (5 mL) chopped fresh parsley
3½ oz (100 g) caul fat
¼ cup (50 mL) butter
1 tbsp (15 mL) olive oil
4 rabbit chops
Spring shoots and edible wild rose
    petals to garnish

MAPLE SUGAR REDUCTION
¼ cup (50 mL) maple sugar
5 tbsp (75 mL) butter
¼ cup (50 mL) fresh orange juice
¼ cup (50 mL) fresh lemon juice
3 tbsp (45 mL) tarragon vinegar
½ cup (125 mL) dark chicken stock
    (see p. 216)
Salt and pepper to taste

To prepare the pineapple butter, skin and core the pineapple, chop into 4 pieces, and boil in a large pot of water until soft. Combine with the butter in a blender and purée until smooth. Set aside.

Peel the white asparagus and add to a pan of water with the butter, salt, and sugar. Boil the asparagus until tender. Cool in ice water.

Roll the rabbit loin in the chopped thyme, tarragon, rosemary, and parsley. Soak the caul fat in lukewarm water for a few minutes, then carefully wrap a strip around each piece of rabbit. Pan-sear in the butter and oil until medium-rare, 2 to 3 minutes, or a little longer if desired. Remove from the pan and set aside. Briefly sear the rabbit chops in the remaining butter until slightly brown, less than a minute.

For the maple sugar reduction, melt the sugar and 4 tbsp (60 mL) of the butter in a saucepan over medium heat to obtain a caramel. Deglaze with the orange juice, lemon juice, and tarragon vinegar. Reduce to a syrup-like consistency. Pour in the dark chicken stock and reduce by three-quarters. Season to taste with salt and pepper. Whisk in the remaining tablespoon of butter.

Cut each piece of loin in half and garnish with spring shoots and edible wild rose petals. Place 2 to 4 pieces of asparagus and 1 tsp (5 mL) pineapple butter on each plate and drizzle with maple sugar reduction.

NOTE: Any good butcher can provide caul fat with a few days' notice. Pork back fat sliced paper-thin can be used as a substitute, but not bacon, for it will impart too much flavour.

Potage of Frogs' Legs with Riesling and Morels

This dish is a classic from Blodelsheim, where I was born. I still remember the old farmers bringing morels to my uncle's restaurant and the kids going to the river to catch frogs. Times are different now, but the soup is still good.

SERVES 4

14 oz (400 g) small frogs' legs

3 tbsp (45 mL) plus $^2/_3$ cup (150 mL) butter

2 tbsp (30 mL) chopped shallots

3 garlic cloves, chopped

½ cup (125 mL) Riesling

2 $^1/_3$ cups (575 mL) chicken stock (see p. 215)

1 $^2/_3$ cups (400 mL) whipping cream

Salt and pepper to taste

$^2/_3$ cup (150 mL) chopped green onions

4 oz (120 g) morel mushrooms

2 tbsp (30 mL) chopped fresh chervil

Remove the small, secondary bone from the frogs' legs and reserve. Scrape the rest toward the base of the main bones to make mini jambonettes.

In a skillet, heat 1 tbsp (15 mL) of the butter and sweat 1 tbsp (15 mL) of the shallots. Add the frogs' leg bones and half the garlic; sauté for a few minutes. Pour in the Riesling and reduce by two-thirds. Stir in the chicken stock and reduce by half. Add the cream and simmer for 5 to 8 minutes. Season with salt and pepper to taste and pass through a fine sieve; set aside.

Add 1 tbsp (15 mL) of the butter, the remaining shallots and garlic, and the green onions to a hot pan. Sauté for a few minutes, then add the frogs' legs. Cook for a few minutes and set aside.

Add 1 tbsp (15 mL) butter and the morels to a hot pan and sauté until softened. Sprinkle with chervil.

Bring the soup to a simmer and with a hand blender, emulsify with the remaining $^2/_3$ cup (150 mL) butter until frothy. Divide the frogs' legs and morels among 4 soup bowls and pour in the frothy liquid.

I love raw meat, but raw baby lamb is an experience unlike any other.

RHUBARB PURÉE
1 stalk (100 g) rhubarb, peeled
   and chopped
2 tbsp (30 mL) sugar
2 tbsp (30 mL) water
½ tsp (2 mL) lemon juice

POACHED RHUBARB
1–2 stalks rhubarb
4 tbsp (60 mL) sugar

BALSAMIC REDUCTION
1¼ cups (300 mL) balsamic vinegar
1 tbsp (15 mL) old-fashioned brown sugar
2 basil leaves
Pinch of salt

LAMB TARTARE
1½-lb (750 g) loin of lamb, cleaned,
   all sinew removed
4 tsp (20 mL) finely diced shallots
4 tsp (20 mL) finely chopped capers
2 tsp (10 mL) finely diced chives
4 tsp (20 mL) olive oil
Salt and pepper to taste
4 quail egg yolks
4 oz (120 g) cold Rondoudou (or other quality)
   ashed goat cheese
Mâche lettuce
½ cup (125 mL) citrus vinaigrette (see p. 226)
Coriander seedlings, grape tomatoes, chives,
   and thinly sliced radish to garnish
1 tbsp (15 mL) balsamic reduction

To make the rhubarb purée, combine the rhubarb, sugar, water, and lemon juice in a saucepan. Cook over medium-low heat, stirring continuously, until soft, approximately 5 minutes. Transfer the mixture to a blender and purée.

Peel and slice the rhubarb stalks into 4-inch (10 cm) pieces. Use a mandoline to slice them into strips. Poach in a saucepan of water and the sugar for 45 seconds. Remove and set aside.

For the balsamic reduction, combine the balsamic vinegar, brown sugar, and basil in a small saucepan and bring to a simmer. Reduce by about a quarter or until the liquid reaches the consistency of a syrup. Pass through a fine sieve and season to taste with salt.

Finely mince the lamb with a chef's knife and mix with the shallots, capers, chives, and olive oil. Season well.

Divide the lamb tartare into 4 servings, shaping it with a 2-inch (5 cm) moulding cylinder if desired. Top each with a quail egg yolk. Thinly slice the goat cheese and arrange around the lamb. Surround with mâche lettuce and poached rhubarb strips; drizzle with citrus vinaigrette. Garnish with coriander seedlings, grape tomatoes, chives, and radish. Drizzle with balsamic reduction and rhubarb purée.

Every year in spring, we breathlessly await the glorious season of sweet spot prawns from the West Coast. Their harvesting time is short—from May through early July—so we try to make the most of it.

SERVES 4

LOBSTER AND SHRIMP
1 1½-lb (750 g) live lobster
½ cup (125 mL) sake
1 tsp (5 mL) chopped fresh coriander
1 grapefruit
1 orange
4 live spot prawns, peeled and sliced
    lengthwise into 2 or 3 strips
Pineapple balls, fresh herbs, and additional
    grapefruit and orange sections to garnish
1 tbsp (15 mL) balsamic reduction (see p. 36)

COCONUT FOAM
2 cups (500 mL) whipping cream
1 14-oz (414 mL) can coconut milk
2 gelatin leaves

CAVIAR VINAIGRETTE
6 tbsp (90 mL) saffron-infused olive oil
Juice of 1 lemon
Salt and pepper
2 tsp (10 mL) caviar

Boil the lobster in water for about 5 minutes, just until the meat separates from the shell. Cool in an ice bath and remove the meat. Marinate in the sake and coriander for 1 hour in the fridge.

Meanwhile, to prepare the coconut foam, combine the cream and coconut milk in a small saucepan and cook over low heat. Soak the gelatin leaves in cold water, drain, and whisk into the cream and milk. Warm the mixture until the leaves dissolve, taking care not to bring it to a boil. Remove from the heat and fill your foam gun (without adding the cap, as the foam needs room to expand). Place in the fridge to cool.

Make the vinaigrette by mixing the oil, lemon juice, salt, and pepper. Sprinkle in the caviar and stir carefully, taking care not to break the eggs. Set aside.

Peel the grapefruit and orange, removing all the pith and membranes so that the flesh is completely exposed. Cut into ½-inch (1 cm) cubes.

Remove the lobster from the sake and cut it into small pieces (about the same size as the fruit). Toss the lobster, grapefruit, and orange together in a bowl and divide into 4 servings. You may wish to shape each serving using a 2½-inch (6 cm) cylinder mould.

Arrange each serving on a plate with the strips of shrimp, 3 tsp (15 mL) of the caviar vinaigrette, and a squirt of the coconut foam. (Hint: You may want to add one or two canisters of CO_2 to your foam gun, depending on how thick you want the foam.) Garnish with pineapple balls, fresh herbs, and grapefruit and orange sections. Drizzle with balsamic reduction.

Two pinches of saffron in 3 tbsp (45 mL) olive oil can be used in place of the saffron-infused olive oil.

Sweetbreads are a favoured offal in France, but were hard to buy in Ontario when I arrived here 15 years ago. Now you can get them at most butcher shops.

SERVES 4

FRIED ZUCCHINI FLOWERS
12 zucchini flowers
1 cup (250 mL) all-purpose flour
Peanut (or other) oil for deep-frying

CHERRY PURÉE
15 cherries, pitted
1 tbsp (15 mL) sherry vinegar
2 tsp (10 mL) organic brown sugar
1 tsp (5 mL) lemon juice

SWEETBREADS
1 lb (500 g) veal sweetbreads, cut into 2-oz (60 g) medallions
1 tbsp (15 mL) granulated maple sugar
Salt and pepper
¼ cup (50 mL) butter or oil

LEEKS
8 wild leeks, bulbs only
4 tbsp (60 mL) chicken stock (see p. 215)
1 tbsp (15 mL) butter
Salt and pepper
Sprouts, black cherries, and maple sugar to garnish

Preheat the oven to 325°F (160°C).

Remove the stamen or pistil from the zucchini flowers and coat well in flour (you can either close the flowers or leave them open). Deep-fry for 1 to 2 minutes in peanut oil, remove carefully from the pan, and set aside.

To prepare the cherry purée, combine the cherries, sherry vinegar, brown sugar, and lemon juice in a small saucepan. Bring to a simmer, ensuring that the sugar is completely melted. Reduce by a quarter, transfer to a blender, and purée until smooth.

Season the sweetbread medallions with the maple sugar, salt, and pepper. Melt the butter in a cast-iron or oven-safe nonstick pan and sear the medallions until they're light brown, taking care not to let the butter turn black. Remove the pan from the heat, place in the oven, and cook for 10 minutes. Meanwhile, combine the leek bulbs, chicken stock, butter, salt, and pepper in a saucepan. Cook over very low heat until everything is reduced and the leeks look glazed, 20 to 30 minutes. The leeks should still have a crunchy texture.

Place 2 sweetbread medallions on each plate on a bed of cherry purée. Arrange 2 or 3 zucchini flowers and 2 leeks around the edges of the plate. Garnish with sprouts, black cherries, maple sugar, and any additional fried zucchini flowers, finely chopped.

NOTE: Try using chopsticks to gently lower the zucchini flowers into the oil and for removing them.

Wild B.C. Salmon with Sorrel and New Brunswick Caviar

As a young chef, I relished my time working at the Dorchester in London. There, I was introduced to the rich flavours of Scotland—the game, lamb, and my favourite, smoked wild salmon. I've added a hint of Canadian innovation to this Old World classic.

SERVES 4

GRATINÉE SAUCE
1 cup (250 mL) beurre blanc (see p. 215)
1 egg yolk
2 tbsp (30 mL) whipped cream

SALMON
1 tbsp (15 mL) butter
Salt and pepper
1½ lb (750 g) salmon, cut into 8 to 12 strips
½ cup (125 mL) sorrel
4 tsp (20 mL) caviar

In a saucepan, heat the beurre blanc and reduce by a quarter. Remove from the heat. In a bowl, whisk the egg yolk with the whipped cream; stir into the beurre blanc, without returning it to the heat. Set aside.

Butter a 3-inch (8 cm) circle on 4 oven-safe serving plates and season the butter with salt and pepper. Arrange 2 to 3 strips of salmon on each plate in a circular shape to form a medallion. Top each medallion with a handful of sorrel and 1 to 2 tbsp (15 to 30 mL) of the sauce. Put under the broiler on very high heat so that the sauce gratinées quickly (the success of the dish depends on the salmon remaining rare inside). Serve immediately with a teaspoon of caviar.

We're lucky in Canada to have an impressive mix of ethnic culinary traditions. This dish marries fantastic Japanese flavours with Canadian ingredients.

SERVES 4

UMEBOSHI MAYONNAISE
2 egg yolks
2 tbsp (30 mL) white wine vinegar
1 tbsp (15 mL) Dijon mustard
½ umeboshi
Juice of ½ lemon
Salt and pepper to taste

SEA URCHIN VINAIGRETTE
2 1-oz (30 g) pieces sea urchin
1 cup (250 mL) walnut oil
½ cup (125 mL) sesame oil
¼ cup (50 mL) rice wine vinegar
2 tsp (10 mL) Dijon mustard

CRAB ROULADE
2 1½-lb (750 g) Dungeness crabs
4 cups (1 L) court bouillon (see p. 224)
½ cucumber
4 tsp (20 mL) caviar
8 cherries, halved
Red shiso leaves and sliced peaches
    to garnish
Salt to taste

To make the umeboshi mayonnaise, blend the egg yolks, white wine vinegar, and Dijon mustard in a food processor for 1 to 2 minutes. Add the umeboshi and lemon juice, blending to a nice, thick consistency. Season to taste.

To prepare the sea urchin vinaigrette, blend the sea urchin, walnut oil, sesame oil, rice wine vinegar, and Dijon mustard in a food processor until smooth and runny. Set aside.

Boil the crab in the court bouillon in a large saucepan for 8 to 10 minutes. Remove the crab and plunge into ice water. When cool, pick the meat from the shells, taking great care not to break the fore claw, and set aside.

Cut the cucumber into 4-inch-long (10 cm), paper-thin strips using a mandoline. Aim for 16 strips (4 per serving). Remove the green skin from one side of each strip and place 4 strips side by side and overlapping (in a "vertical blind" effect) on a piece of plastic wrap. The sides with the skin remaining should be on the outside.

Season the cucumber strips lightly with salt to keep them crisp. Spoon 1½ tsp (7 mL) crab meat in the centre of each "blind" and spread 2 tsp (10 mL) mayonnaise on top. Gently roll the cucumber from the bottom up, using the plastic wrap so that the cucumber forms a roll with the crab and mayonnaise contained within the centre.

Cut each cylinder into 3 pieces and remove the plastic wrap, filling any gaps with additional crab meat. Arrange 3 pieces on each serving plate, along with a teaspoon of caviar and 4 cherry halves. Place any whole meat from the crab claws on top of each serving, top with a teaspoon of umeboshi mayonnaise, and drizzle with the sea urchin vinaigrette. Garnish with red shiso leaves and sliced peaches.

NOTE: Umeboshi is a salt-cured Japanese apricot, available along with red shiso leaves at any good Japanese food store. You may use young basil as a substitute for the shiso.

Lamb Navarin with Chops, Kidneys, Testicles, and Young Fava Beans

Typically, a navarin is a lamb stew. My twist on this classic is to throw in all the "forgotten" parts of the lamb.

SERVES 4
1 cup (250 mL) fava beans

POACHED RHUBARB
½ stalk rhubarb
1½ cups (375 mL) water
1 cup (250 mL) sugar
1 tbsp (15 mL) butter

LAMB
2 tbsp (30 mL) grapeseed oil
¼ cup (50 mL) butter
4 lamb chops (or 1 rack of lamb cut into 4 chops)
2 lamb testicles
1 lamb loin
4 lamb kidneys
4 1-oz (30 g) pieces lamb liver
½ cup (125 mL) lamb jus (see p. 219)
1 sprig of rosemary
1 sprig of thyme
1 roasted garlic bulb, sliced baby zucchini, sliced yellow pattypan squash, and fried sprig of thyme to garnish
1 tbsp (15 mL) olive oil
1 tbsp (15 mL) basil oil (see p. 93)

To prepare the fava beans, remove the beans from the pods and blanch for about 3 minutes. Peel and discard the skins. Set the beans aside.

Prepare the rhubarb by poaching in the water and sugar until al dente, or barely tender. Remove from the pan, cool, and cut into thin strips using a mandoline. Pan-sear the strips in butter until slightly blond; remove from the heat and set aside.

In a frying pan, warm the grapeseed oil with half of the butter over medium heat. Add the chops and sear for 4 minutes or until medium-rare. Add the testicles and the loin. Sear for 2 minutes or until golden brown. Finally, add the kidneys and liver, searing for 1 minute.

In a saucepan, reduce the lamb jus with the rosemary and thyme sprigs by half. Whisk in the rest of the butter and pass the sauce through a fine sieve. Set aside.

Slice the kidneys in half and arrange on 4 serving plates with the chops, testicles, loin, and liver. Divide the fava beans among the plates. Arrange the rhubarb strips around the edges. Garnish with roasted garlic, sliced zucchini and pattypan squash, and fried thyme sprigs. Drizzle with lamb jus, olive oil, and basil oil

The Beretta Farms organic veal we use at our restaurant is delicate and sweet, and finds a beautiful complement in the compelling flavour of crab. The morel sauce links the two tastes.

SERVES 4

CAULIFLOWER PURÉE
1 cup (250 mL) finely chopped cauliflower
1 cup (250 mL) chicken stock (see p. 215)
Pinch of saffron
2 tbsp (30 mL) butter
Salt and pepper

RED WINE REDUCTION
½ cup (125 mL) port
½ cup (125 mL) red wine
1½ cups (375 mL) veal jus (see p. 223)
4 tbsp (60 mL) whipping cream

MOREL ESSENCE
1 tbsp (15 mL) butter
2 shallots, minced
3 oz (90 g) morel mushrooms, washed
    and brushed

VEAL
1 lb veal tenderloin
Salt and pepper
1 tbsp (15 mL) butter
Purple cauliflower, baby carrots, and
    snowpeas, blanched, to garnish

SNOW CRAB CAKES
2 tbsp (30 mL) olive oil
6 green onions, chopped
1½ tsp (7 mL) chopped garlic
1¾ cups (425 mL) bread crumbs
8 oz (225 g) crabmeat
1 egg
1 tbsp (15 mL) mayonnaise
½ tsp (2 mL) ground cayenne pepper
Salt and pepper to taste
½ cup (125 mL) grapeseed oil

To make the cauliflower purée, combine the cauliflower, chicken stock, and saffron in a saucepan. Slowly simmer until the liquid is reduced. Transfer to a blender and add the butter. Season to taste and emulsify until thick. Set aside.

To prepare the red wine reduction, combine the port and red wine in a small saucepan and reduce by just over half. Stir in the veal jus and reduce to half. Add 3 tbsp (45 mL) of the cream and stir well.

In a separate pan, heat the butter and sweat the shallots until translucent. Add the morels and sauté about 4 to 5 minutes longer. Stir the shallots and morels into the red wine sauce.

Season the veal loin well, then pan-sear in butter until medium-rare, taking care to sear *every* side of the loin.

For the crab cakes, heat the olive oil in a skillet over high heat. Sauté the green onions and garlic until tender; transfer to a bowl and cool slightly. Stir in ¾ cup (175 mL) of the bread crumbs, the crabmeat, egg, mayonnaise, cayenne pepper, salt, and pepper. Form into 4 ½-inch (1 cm) thick patties and coat with the remaining bread crumbs. Heat the grapeseed oil in a skillet over medium-high heat. Fry the cakes until golden brown on each side. Drain on paper towels and set aside.

Immediately before serving, stir the remaining tablespoon of cream into the red wine reduction. Cut the veal into 4 pieces and serve each on a bed of the cauliflower purée. Arrange the morels around the veal. Balance the crab cakes on top of the veal. Drizzle with red wine reduction and garnish with purple cauliflower, baby carrots, and snowpeas.

Pieds-Paquets

When I worked in the south of France, all the chefs visited Mme Malet every Wednesday for her famous pieds-paquets. The restaurant was nothing more than a hole in the wall, but her famous dish made dining there a three-star experience.

2 shallots, finely chopped

1 garlic clove, finely chopped

2 tbsp (30 mL) finely chopped parsley

1 tbsp (15 mL) finely chopped thyme

1½ tsp (7 mL) finely chopped oregano

1 lb (500 g) lamb tripe

½ lb (250 g) speck (or lightly smoked bacon), diced

1 cup (250 mL) peeled and sliced carrots

1¾ cups (425 mL) thinly sliced onions

1 tbsp (15 mL) olive oil

6 lamb feet, singed and scrubbed

8½ cups (2.25 L) quartered tomatoes

1 onion stuck with cloves

1 sprig thyme

1 laurel leaf

Sel de Guérande and pepper to taste

5 cups (1.25 L) white wine

1 tbsp (15 mL) butter

Preheat the oven to 275°F (140°C).

Mix together the shallots, garlic, parsley, thyme, and oregano to make a persillade. Cut the tripe into 12 5-inch (12 cm) triangles. Place 1 tsp (5 mL) speck and 1 tsp (5 mL) persillade in the centre of each triangle. Fold the 3 corners of the triangle up to create a parcel and fasten securely with string. You should have 10 to 12 paquets.

Sauté the sliced carrots and onions in the olive oil until browned. Place the lamb feet and paquets as flat as possible in a large roasting pan with a heavy base. Add the sautéed carrots and onions, quartered tomatoes, onion stuck with cloves, thyme, and laurel. Season with salt and pepper. Pour in the white wine and top up with water if necessary to cover the paquets. Cover the pan and cook slowly in the oven for 6 to 7 hours.

Remove the lamb feet and the paquets, setting aside. Bring the sauce to a simmer and reduce for 2 minutes. Whisk in the butter until creamy and thick. Divide the feet and paquets among 4 plates and cover with sauce. Serve hot with boiled potatoes and seasonal vegetables.

NOTE: Herbes de Provence can be used in place of the parsley, thyme, and oregano if desired.

Rhubarb Crumble with Tahitian Vanilla Ice Cream

Can you imagine eating rhubarb for breakfast, lunch, and dinner? I can. When I was a kid, I knew it was springtime when rhubarb ruled the menu. This recipe is one of Maman Jeanne's classics.

SERVES 4

RHUBARB CRUMBLE
8 stalks rhubarb, peeled and chopped
½ cup (125 mL) sugar
4 tbsp (60 mL) Neige cidre de glace
   (or other quality apple ice wine)
½ cup (125 mL) butter
¾ cup (175 mL) all-purpose flour
6 tbsp (90 mL) maple sugar
2 tbsp (30 mL) dried currants
2 tbsp (30 mL) dried cranberries

TAHITIAN VANILLA ICE CREAM
8 egg yolks
¾ cup (175 mL) sugar
2½ cups (625 mL) whipping cream
1½ cups (375 mL) milk
Pinch of salt
2 vanilla bean pods

Preheat the oven to 350°F (180°C).

RHUBARB CRUMBLE
Place the rhubarb, sugar, and Neige cidre de glace in a saucepan over medium heat. Reduce for 10 to 15 minutes.

Meanwhile, using a mixer with the paddle attachment, mix the butter with the flour until it resembles bread crumbs. Stir in the maple sugar, currants, and cranberries.

Pour the stewed rhubarb into an oven-proof dish, scatter the crumble on top, and bake for 10 to 15 minutes.

TAHITIAN VANILLA ICE CREAM
In a mixing bowl, whisk together the egg yolks and sugar.

In a saucepan combine the cream, milk, and salt. Split the vanilla beans in half lengthwise and scrape out the seeds. Add the seeds and pods to the saucepan. Cook over medium heat until the mixture reaches a simmer. Remove from the heat and gradually pour into the yolk mixture, whisking continuously.

Return the mixture to the saucepan and slowly stir over medium heat with a wooden spoon in a figure-eight motion until thickened. The mixture should coat the back of the spoon. Pass through a fine sieve into a bowl surrounded by ice; stir until chilled. Churn in an ice-cream machine according to the manufacturer's directions. Transfer the ice cream to the freezer at least 1 hour before serving.

Place a spoonful of warm rhubarb crumble in the centre of 4 dessert plates and top with a scoop of ice cream. Sprinkle with icing sugar if desired.

Cherry Clafouti

This dessert can be found in every winstub in Alsace in late spring.

SERVES 4

2 lb (1 kg) stoned ripe cherries
¾ cup (175 mL) almond powder
2 tbsp (30 mL) sifted all-purpose flour
¾ cup (175 mL) milk
4 large eggs
²⁄₃ cup (150 mL) sugar
²⁄₃ cup (150 mL) whipping cream
¼ cup (50 mL) melted butter, cooled
1 shot glass of kirsch or amaretto, or
    a few drops of extract of bitter almond
Maple sugar for sprinkling

Preheat the oven to 350°F (180°C).

Place the cherries in a well-buttered 10-inch (25 cm) round mould.

In a mixing bowl, blend the almond powder, flour, and milk. In another bowl, beat the eggs with the sugar. Stir in the cream and the melted butter. Blend in the flour and milk mixture and the kirsch. Pour over the cherries and bake for 35 to 45 minutes. Serve lukewarm sprinkled with maple sugar.

Maple Syrup Gâteau

I love to make this tart for my stores to keep the Canadian maple syrup tradition alive. In fact, it's a staff favourite.

SERVES 4

¼ cup (50 mL) unsalted butter
1 cup (250 mL) maple sugar
Pinch of salt
1 cup (250 mL) maple syrup
3 eggs, beaten
4 tbsp (60 mL) all-purpose flour
1 unbaked tart shell

Preheat the oven to 350°F (180°C).

Whisk the butter until fluffy; gradually add the maple sugar and the salt while continuing to beat. Add the maple syrup, eggs, and flour, mixing well.

Pour the mixture into the tart shell and cook for 35 to 40 minutes or until the blade of a knife inserted in the centre comes out clean. Allow to cool before serving.

Eggs en Cocotte with Smoked Salmon

Nothing satisfies on a Sunday morning like two fresh farm eggs cooked in cream and married with smoked salmon.

SERVES 4

¾ cup (175 mL) whipping cream
2 tsp (10 mL) chopped chives
8 eggs
White pepper and salt to taste
4 slices wild B.C. smoked salmon

Preheat the oven to 375°F (190°C).

Mix the cream and chives. Divide among 4 ramekins. Carefully, without breaking the yolks, crack 2 eggs into each ramekin. Season with salt and pepper.

Place in a bain-marie and bake for 6 to 8 minutes, making sure the yolks stay soft and runny.

Place the ramekins on 4 plates and garnish each with a slice of smoked salmon.

Easter Hot Cross Buns

I first tasted cross buns while working in London. A typical Frenchman, I instantly wondered why we hadn't thought of this great Easter bread first.

SERVES 4

BUNS
2¼ cups (550 mL) all-purpose flour
¼ cup (50 mL) plus ½ tsp (2 mL) sugar
1 tbsp (15 mL) each cinnamon, allspice,
    and ginger
6 tbsp (90 mL) butter, diced
4 tbsp (60 mL) yeast
1¼ cups (300 mL) lukewarm milk
1 egg, beaten
¼ cup (50 mL) currants

CROSSES
4 tbsp (60 mL) all-purpose flour
2 tsp (10 mL) sugar
2 tbsp (30 mL) diced butter
4 tsp (20 mL) ice water

GLAZE
4 tbsp (60 mL) milk
3 tbsp (45 mL) icing sugar

Preheat the oven to 425°F (220°C).

In a stand mixer with the paddle attachment, combine the flour, ¼ cup (50 mL) of the sugar, and the spices. Add the diced butter, stirring until the mixture resembles fine bread crumbs.

Stir the yeast with the lukewarm milk and the remaining ½ tsp (2 mL) sugar. Set aside for 15 minutes. Stir in the egg. Pour into the flour mixture, along with the currants. With the dough hook attachment, knead the dough for a few minutes, adding more flour if it's too sticky. Cover and set aside to rise for 30 to 40 minutes. Divide into 10 to 12 balls.

To make the crosses, combine the flour, sugar, and butter in a bowl. Stir in the ice water to make a firm dough. Roll out about ⅛ inch (3 mm) thick on a floured surface, cut into strips, and brush with a little water. Place the strips on top of the buns, sticky side down, and bake for 10 minutes or until golden brown.

Meanwhile, make the glaze by heating the milk and icing sugar in a small pan until the sugar dissolves. When the buns are done, place them on a cooling rack and brush immediately with the glaze.

Cucumber Jam

I can't rave enough about this jam. It may sound bizarre, but the cucumber sweetness coupled with tingling mint and a hint of vanilla is a taste experience not to be missed.

MAKES 4 MEDIUM-SIZED JARS
3½ cups (875 mL) white sugar
1.8 oz (50 g) yellow pectin
4 cucumbers, peeled, seeded, and cubed
    (2 lb/1 kg in total)
6 fresh mint leaves, chopped
1 vanilla pod
Zest of 2 limes

Stir together the sugar and pectin in a bowl. Combine with the cucumbers, mint, and vanilla in a large saucepan and bring to a boil over medium heat. Simmer for 7 minutes, stirring continuously. Be careful not to cook too long, as overcooking the sugar will produce a caramel.

Grate the lime zest into the pan, giving a final stir before removing from the heat. The liquid should be runny and smooth and retain its green colour. Immediately dispense into warm, sterilized jars while the jam is still hot.

Put the lids and rings on the jars and place them in boiling water, making sure they are covered in at least 2 inches (5 cm) of water. Boil for 5 to 10 minutes. Remove and cool the jars before storing in a dark place in your pantry.

NOTE: Dispensing the jam into jars while it's still hot will prevent mould and better preserve your jam. The jam should last for 3 to 4 years.

Rhubarb, Rose, and Strawberry Jam

When we're not making charcuterie, our next favourite hobby is putting up jars of jam and preserves. It's a time-honoured tradition that I believe is important to keep alive. We've developed a loyal following of young and old who appreciate the wholesome simplicity of these back-to-basics favourites.

MAKES 4 MEDIUM-SIZED JARS

2 lb (1 kg) chopped rhubarb

2 lb (1 kg) very ripe strawberries, hulled

2 lb (1 kg) sugar

6 lemons, juiced and pips set aside

1 lb (500 g) highly scented rose petals, preferably wild

In a large bowl, layer the rhubarb, washed strawberries, and sugar. Pour in the lemon juice, cover, and allow to rest for 6 hours.

Place the rested fruit in a pot (preferably copper), add the lemon pips in a cheesecloth bag, and gently bring to a boil for 5 minutes. Take off the heat and set aside, covered, for another 6 hours.

Add the rose petals to the pot, mixing well with the fruit. Bring to a simmer until the setting point is reached. Take out the lemon pips and pour the hot jam into warm, sterilized jars.

Put the lids and rings on the jars and place them in boiling water, making sure they're covered in at least 2 inches (5 cm) of water. Boil for 5 to 10 minutes. Remove and cool the jars before storing in a dark place in your pantry.

Pickled Wild Leeks

I love wild leeks so much and their season is so short. So, I pickle them. You should too.

MAKES 2 MEDIUM-SIZED JARS

1 cup (250 mL) apple cider vinegar
½ cup (125 mL) sugar
1½ tsp (7 mL) sel de Guérande
1 tsp (5 mL) whole toasted coriander seeds
½ tsp (2 mL) toasted fennel seeds
¼ tsp (1 mL) toasted Szechuan black peppercorns
12 oz (350 g) wild leeks, trimmed and well rinsed

Combine the apple cider vinegar, sugar, sel de Guérande, coriander seeds, fennel seeds, and peppercorns in a saucepan and bring to a boil.

Bring a pot of salted water to a boil. Boil the wild leeks for 2 minutes and cool quickly in ice water. Dry the leeks and place them in sterilized canning jars. Cover with the hot pickling liquid.

Put the lids and rings on the jars and place them in boiling water, making sure they are covered by at least 2 inches (10 cm) of water. Boil for 5 to 10 minutes. Remove and cool the jars before storing in a dark place in your pantry.

SUMMER

Spring is practice for summer—this is the main event. The markets are full, the variety is huge, and everything you see there is in its prime. In summertime, cooking is easy—the only hard part is remembering to keep it simple, because for once the ingredients don't need your help. And that's good because we chefs need all the spare time we can find to stuff as much produce as possible in jars and bottles and cans, to stash in the basement for when it all goes away again.

For me the season starts for real with those perfect little wild strawberries—*fraises des bois*—red right through the centre, sweet and bursting with juice. What are you going to do to improve on that? The cherries, and ripe Niagara fruit, most of all the peaches and apricots—dessert in summer comes as close to pre-made as a chef can stand.

When I was a kid in Alsace I loved being sent down to the garden at the end of the day to collect something for dinner. Greens for the salad, sweet peas, fragrant herbs. But my favourite was the same then as now—those firm, ripe tomatoes that smell of the earth and the sun at the peak of summer. In France we weren't brought up to think much of Italian cooking, but still, the perfect way to eat those tomatoes is sliced thick, with fresh mozzarella, great balsamic, ripe olive oil, and a bit of sea salt.

When I came to Canada, we still had wild Atlantic salmon from the Gaspé from spring to August. Now the only wild salmon is Pacific, and the best is the mid-summer sockeye. It's leaner and flakier than Atlantic salmon, and I like it almost raw, so I always cook it very lightly. The other thing I look forward to is the mid-summer barbecue, and my favourite meat for the grill is a thick rib-eye steak. I dry-age mine for six weeks and the flavour is incredible—especially in summer, when the beef got fattened up the way it's supposed to, eating grass in a field instead of corn in a barn.

BREAKFAST

LUNCH APPETIZER

LUNCH SANDWICH

LUNCH MAIN COURSE

DINNER APPETIZER

Waffles with Summer Fruit and Chantilly Cream

Simply said, my kids adore them!

SERVES 4 TO 6

FRUIT COULIS

2/3 cup (150 mL) fresh sliced strawberries
1/3 cup (75 mL) fresh raspberries
1/3 cup (75 mL) fresh blackberries
1/3 cup (75 mL) fresh blueberries
1/3 cup (75 mL) sugar

CHANTILLY CREAM

1 cup (250 mL) whipping cream
1/4 cup (50 mL) icing sugar

WAFFLES

2 cups (500 mL) all-purpose flour
1 tbsp (15 mL) sugar
1 tbsp (15 mL) baking powder
1 tbsp (15 mL) baking soda
Pinch of salt
2 eggs
1½ cups (375 mL) buttermilk
½ cup (125 mL) whole milk
1/3 cup (75 mL) melted butter
Fresh mint leaves, icing sugar, and
    additional fresh berries to garnish

To make the coulis, combine the strawberries, raspberries, blackberries, and blueberries in a small saucepan with the sugar. Keeping the heat low, bring to a slow boil and simmer gently, stirring occasionally, until the sugar melts completely and a nice compote remains. Don't overcook the fruit. The berries should retain their shape once the sugar has melted.

Next, prepare the Chantilly cream by beating the whipping cream in a bowl until stiff. Slowly add the icing sugar, beating until the sugar disappears. Take care not to overbeat or your cream will turn to butter. Set aside.

To make the waffles, sift the flour, sugar, baking powder, baking soda, and salt into a large bowl. In another large mixing bowl, whisk the eggs, buttermilk, and whole milk. Slowly add the melted butter, whisking continuously. Fold in the flour mixture, whisking continuously. Once all the ingredients are combined, use a spatula to stir until the batter is smooth and runny, taking care not to overmix or the batter will become dough.

Preheat your waffle iron to full power and lubricate the plates with butter or oil. Fill with a generous amount of batter—an 8-inch (20 cm) iron will use about a third of the batter. Close and cook for about 4 minutes or until the waffle is golden brown with crispy edges. The centre should be soft. Note: The second waffle you make will almost always be best.

Cut each waffle into quarters (if necessary) and place two quarters on each serving plate. Top one of the waffle quarters with a tablespoon of the fruit compote and lean the second quarter against the fruit. Top with a teaspoon of the Chantilly cream and garnish with mint leaves, sifted icing sugar, and additional fresh fruit if desired.

NOTE   An 8-inch (20 cm) waffle iron will make 3 large waffles.

Chilled Cucumber Soup with Caviar and Wild B.C. Smoked Salmon Roll

Wild salmon are enigmatic and magical creatures. First Nations people have traditionally enjoyed a close relationship with the king of all fish—aka wild B.C. salmon—for food as well as ceremonial celebrations. For a chef, wild salmon should always have a prestigious place on the menu.

SERVES 4

CUCUMBER SOUP

3 large cucumbers, peeled, seeded, and chopped
4 tbsp (60 mL) chopped mint
2 tbsp (30 mL) chopped dill
1 garlic clove, chopped
1 shallot, chopped
2 cups (500 mL) plain yogurt
1 cup (250 mL) sour cream
Salt and pepper to taste

SMOKED SALMON ROLL

Skin of 3–4 cucumbers
½ cup (125 mL) sour cream
4 tbsp (60 mL) caviar
8–10 slices smoked salmon

To prepare the soup, combine the cucumber, mint, dill, garlic, shallot, yogurt, and sour cream in a blender; purée until smooth. Season to taste. Cool in the fridge for 30 minutes.

Meanwhile, peel the cucumber, slice it into 3-inch sections, and using a mandoline slice them lengthwise to create 3-inch-long strips.

Place the strips on a sheet of plastic wrap or a chopping board, arranging them vertically in an overlapping row. Spread with a thin layer of sour cream, followed by a thin layer of caviar. Layer the salmon slices across the caviar. Then neatly roll up the strip in the plastic wrap and twist the ends to hold. Store in the refrigerator for 30 minutes to set, and then quarter the rolls, peel off the plastic wrap, and serve as a side to the soup.

NOTE Cucumber jam is superb with this recipe (see p. 63).

Sliced Peaches and Melon Balls with Prosciutto

Late afternoon in sunny Tuscany is the ideal setting for this dish. Imagine an old wooden table set on a terrace overlooking a vineyard. Or simply relax in your own garden and bring the taste of Tuscany to you.

SERVES 4 TO 6

5–7 varieties of melon (such as red and yellow watermelon,
    Santa Claus, honeydew, marsh, canary, and crenshaw)
3 peaches
Fresh mint, garden herbs, and baby arugula leaves to garnish
12–14 slices prosciutto

Ball the melons using a ¾-inch (19 mm) melon baller (or whatever you have at home). Thinly slice the peaches using a mandoline.

On each serving plate, place about 5 melon balls on a peach slice and repeat the layers to create a tower of about 3 layers. Top the final layer of melon balls with a folded peach slice, mint, and your choice of garden herb. Surround each tower with 2 or 3 slices of prosciutto and garnish with a few baby arugula leaves.

NOTE. For a variation, substitute heirloom tomatoes for the melon.

Chilled Melon Soup with Feta and Melon Balls

Forget a cold beer on a hot afternoon—this is even more refreshing.

SERVES 4

4 cups chopped marsh melon (approx. 1 melon)
Juice of 1 lemon
Juice and grated zest of 1 lime
¼ cup (50 mL) port
4 slices Canadian feta (8 oz/225 g in total)
Assorted melon balls to garnish

Purée the melon, lemon juice, lime juice and zest, and port in a blender until runny and smooth. Serve with a slice of feta and melon balls for garnish.

NOTE   For added colour and flavour, use different varieties of melon for the garnish.

Heirloom Tomatoes with Roasted Peppers, Toasted Garlic Bread, and Balsamic Vinaigrette

Taste a piece of history. Once mistakenly considered poisonous by the Europeans, the tomato has since graced millions of kitchens. I think this is the best salad in the world.

SERVES 4

BALSAMIC VINAIGRETTE
1 cup (250 mL) olive oil
4 tbsp (60 mL) balsamic vinegar
1 tsp (5 mL) chopped garlic
¼ cup (50 mL) lemon juice
Pinch of salt

GARLIC BREAD
4 slices sourdough bread
¼ cup (50 mL) butter
2 garlic cloves

SALAD
2 red bell peppers
2 yellow bell peppers
¼ cup (50 mL) canola oil
2 tbsp (30 mL) olive oil
1 tbsp (15 mL) balsamic vinegar
1 tsp (5 mL) julienne of basil
Salt and pepper
6 heirloom tomatoes (2 yellow, 2 red, 2 purple)
8 cherry tomatoes
Garden herbs to garnish

Preheat the oven to 350°F (180°C).

To make the vinaigrette, whisk the oil, balsamic vinegar, garlic, and lemon juice in a bowl. Add a pinch of salt to taste and set aside.

In a nonstick pan, toast the bread in the butter and garlic (taking care not to burn the garlic) until the bread is golden brown.

Toss the red and yellow peppers in the canola oil and roast whole until the skin is brown and can be peeled (15 to 20 minutes). Meanwhile, combine the olive oil, balsamic vinegar, basil, salt, and pepper in a bowl and mix well. Cool, peel, and cut each pepper into quarters, ensuring all seeds and stalks are removed, then toss in the oil mixture.

Wash and slice the tomatoes (halve the cherry tomatoes) and divide equally among 4 plates, adding a piece of toasted bread and 2 pieces of pepper to each serving. Arrange in decorative manner, drizzle with the balsamic vinaigrette, and garnish with your choice of garden herbs.

Stewed Chinook Salmon with Peach, Plum, and Blackcurrant Salad, Banyuls Vinaigrette, and Avocado Coulis

If you can find it, buy it. The exceptional flavour of the Chinook salmon is the crown on this dish. Coupled with seasonal fresh fruit, it makes this salad a memorable meal.

SERVES 4

COULIS
1 ripe unblemished avocado
Juice of 2 limes
1 tbsp (15 mL) carbonated water
Salt and pepper to taste

VINAIGRETTE
¼ cup (50 mL) Banyuls vinegar
2 tsp (10 mL) Dijon mustard
Juice of 1 lime
Salt and pepper to taste
½ cup (125 mL) peanut oil

SALMON
4 4-oz (120 g) skinless Chinook salmon fillets
3 pluots (plum-apricots)
3 peaches
1 cup (250 mL) blackcurrants
Garden herbs to garnish
4 tsp (20 mL) caviar (optional)

To prepare the avocado coulis, peel and finely chop the avocado. Add the lime juice, a splash of carbonated water, and a pinch of salt and pepper; mix in a blender until smooth and runny. Set aside.

Next, make the vinaigrette by whisking the vinegar and mustard in a mixing bowl. Add the lime juice, salt, and pepper. Slowly mix in the peanut oil until the desired consistency is achieved.

Steam the salmon steaks until medium-rare, 3 to 4 minutes. Quarter the steaks and arrange the cubes on 4 serving plates with a teaspoon of the avocado coulis. Halve, core, and thinly slice the pluots and peaches and arrange decoratively around the salmon and coulis. Use any leftover peaches to make small peach balls and scatter, together with a handful of blackcurrants, around the salmon. Drizzle with the Banyuls vinaigrette and garnish with your choice of garden herbs. Top each serving of salmon with a teaspoon of caviar if desired.

NOTE: Banyuls vinegar is a golden-coloured wine vinegar from the Banyuls-sur-Mer region of France. Aged in oak barrels for at least five years, it has a sweet, nutty flavour. If it's unavailable, sherry or red wine vinegar may be used instead.

Niçoise Salad

I used to use bluefin, but because it's endangered I now use yellowfin.

2 3½-oz (100 g) yellowfin tuna steaks

1 egg white, beaten

2 cups (500 mL) panko bread crumbs

2 tbsp (30 mL) canola oil

12 fingerling potatoes

2 cups (500 mL) green beans

10 quail eggs

16 olives (assorted, marinated in oil)

8 caper berries

2 cups (500 mL) heirloom cherry tomatoes

1 tbsp (15 mL) red wine vinegar

Salad leaves to garnish

To prepare the tuna, dip the steaks in the egg white and toss in the panko, making sure to coat each side. Warm the canola oil in a nonstick or cast-iron pan. On very high heat, sear the tuna on each side until golden brown on the edges, about 2 minutes per side. The centre should remain raw.

Boil the potatoes until soft; cool, halve, and set aside. Blanch the green beans by boiling for 2 minutes then plunging into an ice bath until cool. This will retain their colour and crunchy texture.

Meanwhile, soft-boil the quail eggs (about 2 minutes), carefully remove from the pan using a slotted spoon, and place in ice water. When cool, peel carefully, halve, and set aside. The eggs should be soft with a runny yolk.

Halve the tuna steaks and divide the pieces among 4 serving plates (you may want to slice each half). Accompany with 4 olives, 6 potato halves, 2 caper berries, a handful of green beans (split, if desired), and a selection of cherry tomatoes. Drizzle with red wine vinegar and garnish with your choice of salad leaves.

NOTE: To seal the flavour when searing the tuna, give the steak a quick flash over high heat on each side so that the centre remains raw and a nice change in colour can be seen from outside to centre when the steak is cut.

Focaccia Panini with Chicken, Oven-Dried Tomatoes, Bocconcini, and Baby Arugula

This makes an excellent Sunday lunch with leftover chicken. Remember to prepare the oven-dried tomatoes the night before; if you forget, use store-bought sun-dried tomatoes.

MAKES 4 SANDWICHES

8 tomatoes
Salt and pepper
2 tbsp (30 mL) olive oil
8 slices focaccia bread, buttered
½ cup (125 mL) chopped fresh basil
Small packet (approx. 8 oz/225 g) bocconcini, thinly sliced
2 cups (500 mL) baby arugula
12–16 slices cooked chicken breast

To oven-dry the tomatoes, cut in half, season with salt and pepper, and toss in the olive oil. Bake in the oven overnight at 100°F (35°C) or at the lowest temperature setting on your oven.

Sprinkle the focaccia slices with the chopped basil. Cover one side with a few slices of bocconcini and top with arugula and oven-dried tomatoes (4 halves per sandwich). Add 3 to 4 slices of the chicken and season well.

Put the two sides together and cook in a panini press until the cheese is melted. Cut in half and serve.

Canadian Wagyu Bavette with Fries, Bone Marrow, and Shallot Reduction

Patrick and Kimberley McCarthy championed the raising of Wagyu cattle in Camrose, Alberta, and introduced me to their remarkable venture. Kudos to them for succeeding in farming something so time-honoured and inherent to Japanese culture and providing us with such a magnificently marbled meat. It's a luxury to prepare this classic bavette dish with a piece of meat this tender.

SERVES 4

MARROW
4 2-inch (5 cm) pieces Wagyu shank bone marrow
Salt and pepper to taste

FRENCH FRIES
4 medium potatoes
2–3 cups (500–750 mL) peanut oil

STEAKS
½ cup (125 mL) butter
4 7-oz (200 g) bavettes (hanger steaks)
Salt and pepper to taste

SHALLOT AND RED WINE SAUCE
4 shallots, thinly sliced
½ cup (125 mL) butter
1 cup (250 mL) port
1 cup (250 mL) red wine
2 cups (500 mL) veal jus (see p. 223)

Preheat the oven to 350°F (180°C).

Soak the marrow bones in lukewarm water for 24 hours, changing the water at least 4 times. Dry the bones with a cloth, season well, and wrap in foil. Cook in the oven for 10 minutes or until the marrow is soft.

To prepare the fries, wash and peel the potatoes, cut in thin strips, and soak in cold water for at least an hour. Dry thoroughly with dish towels. Blanch in the peanut oil on low heat (250°F/120°C) until soft, 4 to 5 minutes. Set aside to cool. Return the fries to the oil and cook on high heat (350–400°F/180–200°C) until golden brown and crispy.

To cook the bavettes, melt the butter in a medium or large pan. Season the bavettes on both sides and fry over medium heat for 3 to 4 minutes per side to cook the steaks rare. Remove the bavettes and allow to rest for 10 minutes while you prepare the sauce.

Sauté the shallots in 2 tbsp (30 mL) of the butter in a small pan until slightly browned. Deglaze with the port and red wine over high heat and reduce to a syrupy consistency, being careful not to burn (approx. 5 minutes). Pour in the veal jus and reduce by half. Whisk in the remaining butter. Set aside.

Serve the bavettes sliced with a few spoonfuls of sauce, fries, and bone marrow.

NOTE You may want to prepare the bone marrow in advance to save time.

Grilled Organic Veal Chop with Chanterelles, Summer Vegetables, and Parmesan Cream

I owned Centro Grill and Wine Bar in Toronto for 13 years. During that time, I felt that I perfected this dish—taking it off the menu would have caused a revolution and culinary pandemonium in the restaurant.

SERVES 4

4 cups (1 L) chicken stock (see p. 215)
4 yellow baby carrots, 1 inch (2.5 cm) of
    greens attached
4 orange baby carrots
8 medium spring onions, trimmed and peeled
4 baby turnips, peeled, 1 inch (2.5 cm)
    of greens attached
4 baby zucchini
4 baby yellow zucchini

1 lb (500 g) chanterelle mushrooms, cleaned
½ cup (125 mL) grapeseed oil
5 tbsp (75 mL) unsalted butter
Salt and pepper to taste
2 large veal rib chops, trimmed
4 tbsp (60 mL) whipping cream
¼ tsp (1 mL) lemon juice
1 tbsp (15 mL) Parmigiano-Reggiano
¼ cup (50 mL) baby spinach, washed

In a medium saucepan, bring 3 cups (750 mL) of the chicken stock to a simmer; add the yellow and orange carrots and cook until tender. Using a slotted spoon, transfer the carrots to a large, shallow pot. Cook the onions, turnips, and then zucchini separately in the same stock, adding them to the pot with the carrots as they become tender. Do not discard the stock.

In a large skillet, sauté the chanterelle mushrooms over high heat in ¼ cup (50 mL) of the grapeseed oil. When the mushrooms are softened, add 1 tbsp (15 mL) of the butter, making sure the butter doesn't burn. Season to taste, remove from heat, and set aside.

In a large skillet, heat the remaining ¼ cup (50 mL) grapeseed oil over medium heat. Season the veal chops on both sides with salt and pepper and place in the skillet.

Turn the chops once while basting frequently until golden brown, 6 to 8 minutes on each side. At about half the cooking time, add 1 tbsp (15 mL) of the butter to help with the basting. When cooked, transfer the chops to a wire rack to rest for 15 minutes.

Bring the reserved cup of chicken stock to a simmer. Reduce by three-quarters and add the cream. Reduce until the sauce coats the back of a spoon. Whisk in the remaining 3 tbsp (45 mL) butter and season to taste with salt, pepper, and lemon juice. With a hand blender, froth the sauce, and sprinkle in the Parmigiano. Add the sauce to the reserved vegetables over medium heat (taking care the sauce doesn't boil) until the vegetables are heated through. Warm the mushrooms over low heat and place the spinach leaves on top until wilted.

Spoon the vegetables, mushrooms, and spinach attractively in the centre of 4 serving plates. Place the veal chops on top and serve immediately.

Méli-Mélo of Tartare "Sea, Earth, and Sky"

I paint in my spare time. It keeps me sane—if such a word could ever be used to describe me. I first created the colours and the vibrancy of this dish on canvas, and felt compelled to transfer them to the plate.

SERVES 4

3 oz (90 g) scallops, diced
2 tsp (10 mL) olive oil
2 tsp (10 mL) summer truffle, chopped
1 tsp (5 mL) lemon juice
Garnishes: 2 tsp (20 mL) caviar,
    frisée sprigs

3 oz (90 g) beef tenderloin, diced
2 tsp (10 mL) olive oil
1 tsp (5 mL) aged red wine vinegar
½ tsp (2 mL) chopped capers
Salt and pepper
Garnishes: diced pineapple, beet cress

3 oz (90 g) raw duck, diced
1 tsp (5 mL) teriyaki sauce
½ tsp (2 mL) sesame oil
½ tsp (2 mL) pickled Japanese ginger
Salt and pepper
Garnishes: Thinly sliced gingerroot,
    blackcurrants, cress, thinly sliced
    heirloom cherry tomatoes

3 oz (90 g) cooked crab meat, picked over
2 tsp (10 mL) mayonnaise
Pinch of chopped lime leaves
1 tsp (5 mL) pickled Japanese ginger
Salt and pepper
Garnish: 4 tsp (20 mL) whitefish caviar

3 oz (90 g) wild sockeye salmon
2 tsp (10 mL) olive oil
1 tsp (5 mL) lime juice
Zest of ½ lime
Garnishes: thinly sliced green grapes,
    thinly sliced radishes

3 oz (90 g) roasted red pepper, diced
2 tsp (10 mL) olive oil
1 tsp (5 mL) balsamic vinegar
Salt and pepper
Garnishes: thinly sliced or grated heirloom
    carrots, heirloom cherry tomatoes

3 oz (90 g) roasted orange pepper, diced
2 tsp (10 mL) olive oil
1 tsp (5 mL) balsamic vinegar
Salt and pepper
Garnishes: red beet, sliced in thin strips
    or grated

¾ oz (20 g) toro (tuna belly)
Fleur de sel (sea salt)
Garnishes: pickled gingerroot, shiso leaves,
    peeled, thinly sliced candied beet

ADDITIONAL GARNISHES
Beet reduction, cloudberry coulis, coriander
    and basil oil, preserved peach, squashberry
    green tea jelly, thinly sliced plum, beet cress,
    thin melon batons (available at fine food stores)

IN SEPARATE BOWLS

Mix the scallops with the olive oil, summer truffle, and lemon juice. Mix the diced beef with the olive oil, vinegar, capers, salt, and pepper. Mix the duck with the teriyaki sauce, sesame oil, and pickled gingerroot. Mix the crab with the mayonnaise, lime leaves, pickled ginger, salt, and pepper.

Marinate the salmon in the olive oil, lime juice, and lime zest for 10 minutes. Marinate the red and orange peppers separately in the olive oil, balsamic vinegar, salt, and pepper. Cut the toro into 4 squares of equal size and season with sea salt.

Divide the scallops, beef, duck, crab, and red and orange peppers into 4 equal servings (approx. ¾ oz/20 g per serving), taking care to keep all the components separate. Using a 1- to 1½-inch (2 to 4 cm) mould, shape each serving carefully and arrange across 4 serving plates. Cut the salmon into 4 strips and arrange each strip in a medallion on the plates. Add the seasoned toro squares.

Top each serving with the appropriate garnish, then drizzle each plate with beet reduction, cloudberry coulis, and coriander and basil oil. Add 1 tsp (5 mL) preserved peach and ¼ tsp (1 mL) squashberry green tea jelly to each plate, and garnish with thin melon batons.

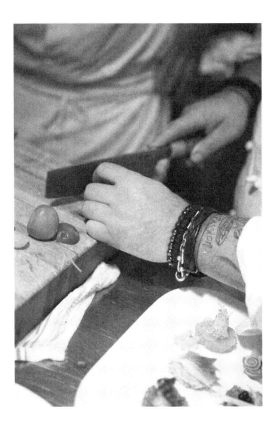

Sockeye Salmon and Toro Belly
Sashimi, Cantaloupe Melon, Avocado
Cream, and Soy Vinaigrette

The colour and flavour of the sockeye salmon is unbeatable. Ever since I started cooking in Canada, the wait for the salmon run, for me, has been like a kid waiting for Santa at Christmas.

SERVES 4

AVOCADO CREAM

1 avocado, peeled and pitted
3 tbsp (45 mL) whipping cream
1 tbsp (15 mL) lemon juice
Salt and pepper to taste

SOY VINAIGRETTE

½ cup (125 mL) sake
½ cup (125 mL) mirin (sweet cooking wine)
½ cup (125 mL) soy sauce
½ cup (125 mL) honey

BEET REDUCTION

4 medium red beets, peeled and juiced
   (or 1 cup/250 mL fresh beet juice)

SASHIMI

1–2 (600 g) raw sockeye salmon skinless fillets
4 oz (120 g) toro (tuna belly)
Half a honeydew melon
Half a cantaloupe melon
Heirloom carrots and yellow beets, grated or thinly
   sliced using a mandoline, frisée, beet cress,
   shiso chiffonade, and blackberries to garnish

To make the avocado cream, purée the avocado, cream, and lemon juice in a blender until smooth. Season to taste and set aside. Make the soy vinaigrette by combining the sake, mirin, soy sauce, and honey in a saucepan. Bring to a boil over medium heat and reduce to a syrupy consistency. Set aside to cool. To make the reduction, transfer beet juice to a simmer over low heat and reduce gently by at least three-quarters, until it thickens to syrup. Cool in the refrigerator.

Slice the salmon fillets into ½-inch by 2-inch (1 cm by 5 cm) strips. You'll need 3 strips per serving. Using the salmon strips to measure, cut the toro and honeydew and cantaloupe melons into identical strips, retaining any surplus melon for use as garnish.

On each serving plate, layer a strip of salmon on top of a strip of honeydew. Layer a strip of toro on top of a strip of the cantaloupe. Place an additional strip of melon on each plate and layer with half a strip of salmon and half a strip of toro (halved lengthwise, each 5 mm/¼ inch wide).

Using a ¾-inch (19 mm) baller, create melon balls from any additional melon and scatter across the dishes. Garnish with the heirloom carrots, yellow beets, shiso leaves, frisée, beet cress, and blackberries.

Drizzle with the soy vinaigrette and about 1 tbsp (15 mL) of the beet reduction and serve with a teaspoon of avocado cream.

NOTE: Shiso leaves are found in Japanese groceries. If unavailable, substitute fresh basil or mint leaves.

Steak Tartare

Steak tartare is traditionally made with horse meat, which is the way I prefer it. But you'll typically find it made with beef and it's just as good.

SERVES 4

13 oz (375 g) lean beef tenderloin
4 egg yolks
4 tsp (20 mL) finely diced shallots
1 tsp (5 mL) finely diced capers
1 tsp (5 mL) finely diced gherkin
1 tsp (5 mL) Dijon mustard
1 tsp (5 mL) ketchup
2 tsp (10 mL) Worcestershire sauce
1 tsp (5 mL) Tabasco sauce
4 tsp (20 mL) chopped chives
Salt and white pepper to taste
4 quail eggs

Finely mince the beef tenderloin and in a large mixing bowl combine with egg yolks, shallots, capers, gherkin, Dijon mustard, ketchup, Worcestershire sauce, Tabasco sauce, and chopped chives. Fold the mixture to mix thoroughly. Season to taste.

Divide into 4 servings and shape using a mould if desired. Cut the tops off the quail eggs, separate, and return the yolks to the shells. Place on top of the tartare for garnish.

Terrine of Buffalo Mozzarella and Heirloom Tomatoes with Basil Oil and Balsamic Syrup

This is my take on the Italian classic insalata Caprese. Being a true Frenchman, I put it in a terrine.

SERVES 4

BASIL OIL
1 cup (250 mL) fresh basil leaves, blanched
1½ cups (375 mL) extra-virgin olive oil

BALSAMIC SYRUP
1½ cups (375 mL) balsamic vinegar
¼ cup (50 mL) old-fashioned brown sugar

TERRINE
9 large heirloom tomatoes
4 gelatin leaves
4 large buffalo mozzarella balls
1 bunch fresh basil
Pinch of sel de Guérande or Fleur de sel
Niçoise olives and roasted peppers
    to garnish (optional)

To make the basil oil, blend the basil leaves and olive oil on high speed in a blender. Pour into a dish, cover, and refrigerate for 4 days. Strain through cheesecloth and pour into a squeeze bottle.

For the balsamic syrup, mix the balsamic vinegar and brown sugar in a small saucepan and bring to a simmer. Reduce heat to medium and simmer until reduced to ¾ cup (175 mL).

To prepare the terrine, cut 4 of the tomatoes into 1-inch (2.5 cm) squares. Place the squares in a blender and purée until smooth. Strain through cheesecloth and set the liquid aside.

Soak the gelatin leaves in ample water for 15 minutes or until soft. Squeeze all the liquid from the gelatin, heat up the tomato water, and add the drained gelatin leaves. Whisk until dissolved.

Slice the remaining tomatoes into ¼-inch (5 mm) slices. Lay on towels and press to absorb extra moisture. Thinly slice the buffalo mozzarella and pat dry. Line a 4- by 12-inch loaf pan with plastic wrap. Layer the tomatoes, mozzarella, and basil leaves and brush the tomato water on each layer. Seal with plastic wrap and cover with foil. Weigh down the terrine with something heavy, such as cans or a brick. Refrigerate for at least 3 days to allow the terrine to set.

Unmould onto a cutting board. Carefully, with an electric knife, cut the terrine into 1-inch (2.5 cm) slices.

Place the slices in the centre of 4 plates and tastefully drizzle the basil oil and the balsamic syrup around the terrine. Sprinkle the terrine with sel de Guérande. Garnish the plates with Niçoise olives and roasted peppers, if desired.

Tuna Belly, Carpaccio of Peaches, Seaweed Purée, and Egg Dressing

I always appreciate the luxury of incorporating something from my own backyard into a dish that's immensely popular halfway around the world. With this toro sashimi, I use my favourite peaches, from the Niagara region.

SERVES 4

EGG DRESSING
2 egg yolks
2 tsp (10 mL) sesame oil
2 tsp (10 mL) soy sauce
Pinch of salt

SEAWEED PURÉE
2 sheets nori (dried seaweed sheets)
3 cups (750 mL) dashi (seaweed stock)
1 tsp (5 mL) mirin (sweet cooking wine)

TUNA AND PEACHES
2 peaches, halved and thinly sliced
4 oz (120 g) toro (tuna belly)
1 tbsp (15 mL) coriander oil or other green oil
    (basil, chive, onion)
Shiso leaves, frisée, summer herbs,
    beet stem, and radishes to garnish
4 tsp (20 mL) wasabi

Prepare the vinaigrette by whisking together the egg yolks, sesame oil, and soy sauce until mixture is light and runny. Add salt to taste and set aside.

To make the seaweed purée, soak the nori sheets in water, preferably overnight. Drain and add the nori to a saucepan with the dashi. Bring to a boil and reduce by three-quarters over medium heat. Add the mirin and further reduce until a paste-like consistency is achieved.

Arrange the peach slices in fan-like shapes across 4 serving plates. Divide the tuna belly into 4 servings, then cut each serving into cubes and arrange around the peaches. Drizzle with the egg yolk dressing and coriander oil. Garnish with shiso leaves, frisée, summer herbs, beet stem, and radishes. Serve each plate with a teaspoon of wasabi and a teaspoon of seaweed purée.

NOTE: All ingredients are available from Japanese supermarkets and fine food stores.

Minted Summer Pea Froth with Digby Scallops and Caviar Tian

The beauty of summer is found in the vibrantly coloured fruits and vegetables of the season. Potage Saint-Germain has been my favourite soup since I was a kid. Below is my version of this wonderful classic paired with tender and sweet Digby Bay scallops.

SERVES 4

SCALLOPS
4 Digby scallops
8 tsp (40 mL) caviar

BROTH
1 tbsp (15 mL) finely chopped onion
1 tsp (5 mL) minced garlic
2 cups (500 mL) garden peas
4 mint leaves (preferably wild)
1 cup (250 mL) chicken stock
   (see p. 215)
½ cup (125 mL) whipping cream
2 tbsp (30 mL) butter
2 tbsp (30 mL) whipped cream
Salt and pepper to taste
Chopped mint leaves to garnish
4 tsp (20 mL) coconut foam
   (see p. 37), optional

Lightly torch the sea scallops for 3 seconds on each side to firm up the skin. Cut each scallop widthwise into 3 slices. Reassemble the scallops, adding a teaspoon of caviar between each piece to form layers. Set aside.

To prepare the broth, sauté the onion and garlic over medium heat until slightly coloured, then add the peas, mint leaves, and chicken stock. Bring to a simmer for 5 to 7 minutes and stir in the whipping cream.

Transfer the mixture to a blender and purée until smooth. Pass through a fine sieve and return to the saucepan. Warm over medium heat, then mix in the butter and whipped cream. Stir well, heating until the butter is completely melted. Season to taste and sprinkle with chopped mint leaves.

Distribute the broth among 4 bowls and serve with a scallop tian and a teaspoon of coconut foam.

Canadian Wagyu is so rich and succulent that when paired with potatoes fried in duck fat, it reaches an almost ethereal level of gluttony. If you can't find Wagyu steaks, use the most marbled, dry-aged Black Angus you can find.

SERVES 4

FRIED POTATOES
5 lb (2.5 kg) large potatoes
Duck fat, for deep-frying
Sel de Guérande to taste
2 tbsp (30 mL) unsalted butter

BEEF
½ cup (125 mL) cracked Szechuan peppercorns
2 2½-lb (1.25 kg) Canadian Wagyu rib steaks, on the bone
2 tbsp (30 mL) olive oil
4 tbsp (60 mL) unsalted butter

SHALLOT SAUCE
2 tbsp (30 mL) unsalted butter, cut into small cubes
5 shallots, finely chopped
¼ cup (50 mL) cognac
¼ cup (50 mL) port
2 cups (500 mL) veal jus (see p. 223)
Fine sea salt and freshly ground pepper to taste

Peel the potatoes and cut into ½-inch (1 cm) sticks. Melt the duck fat in a large, deep, heavy skillet. You should have at least 4 inches (10 cm) of fat in the skillet. Heat until very hot. Pat the potatoes dry and fry in batches, turning occasionally, until golden brown (10 to 12 minutes). Drain on paper towels and season with the sel de Guérande. In a large frying pan over medium heat, melt the butter and add the potatoes. Toss. Season to taste and set aside.

Spread the cracked Szechuan peppercorns on a plate. Coat the beef steaks with the olive oil and press into the peppercorn. In a large cast-iron pan over medium heat, heat 3 tbsp (45 mL) of the butter until golden. Add the beef to the pan and brown all sides. Add the remaining tablespoon of butter and cook, basting often, for 7 to 8 minutes per side. Place on a wire rack and let rest for 10 minutes.

To make the sauce, drain all the fat from the pan and add 1 tbsp of the cubed butter. Cook the shallots over medium heat until translucent. Deglaze the pan with cognac and port, simmering until reduced by half. Add the veal jus and reduce by half again.

Strain the sauce through cheesecloth and return the liquid to the saucepan over medium heat while whisking in the remaining butter cubes. Season to taste and keep warm.

Arrange the potatoes around the beef in the middle of a serving platter. Pour the sauce into a sauceboat. The beef should be sliced at the table.

Slow-Roasted Pacific Halibut with Potato Scale, Chanterelles, and Red Wine Reduction

For me, preparing and presenting this dish is a lot of fun. Enjoy the act of dressing this fish. Enjoy eating it.

SERVES 4

RED WINE REDUCTION
2 tbsp (30 mL) butter
1 tbsp (15 mL) chopped shallots
½ cup (125 mL) red wine vinegar
2 cups (500 mL) fish stock (see p. 216)
2 cups (500 mL) red wine
1 cup (250 mL) port

POTATOES
2 cups (500 mL) clarified butter
8 fingerling potatoes, peeled
Salt and pepper to taste

MUSHROOMS
2 tbsp (30 mL) grapeseed oil
1 lb (500 g) chanterelle
   mushrooms, cleaned
1 tsp (5 mL) chopped chervil
Salt and pepper to taste

HALIBUT
4 8-oz (225 g) pavés (skinless fillets)
   of Pacific halibut
Sel de Guérande to taste
1 tbsp (15 mL) butter

Preheat the oven to 375°F (190°C).

To make the red wine reduction, melt 1 tbsp (15 mL) of the butter in a saucepan and cook the shallots until translucent. Deglaze with the red wine vinegar and reduce until nearly dry. Add the fish stock and reduce by half. Stir in the red wine and port and reduce by approximately a quarter. Set aside.

For the potatoes, heat the clarified butter in a saucepan over medium heat, but don't allow it to simmer. With a mandoline, thinly slice the potatoes to obtain small discs. Cook for 1 minute in the hot clarified butter. Carefully remove the discs and place them on a tray lined with parchment paper, overlapping to suggest fish scales. Make 4 squares the same size as the fish fillets. Gently brush the potato scales with a little more clarified butter and season with salt and pepper. Bake for 10 to 15 minutes or until golden. Remove from the oven and set aside.

Heat the grapeseed oil in a frying pan on medium heat and add the mushrooms. Sauté for a few minutes and stir in the chopped chervil; season with salt and pepper. Cook for a few more minutes or until the mushrooms soften. Set aside on paper towels.

Season the fish with sel de Guérande. In a skillet over medium heat, melt the tablespoon of butter and slowly cook the pavés for 3 to 4 minutes on each side until golden. Set aside.

Just before serving, bring the red wine reduction back to a simmer and slowly whisk in the remaining 1 tbsp (15 mL) butter. Season to taste.

Place the mushrooms on top of the fish in the centre of 4 plates. Top with the potato scales and pour the red wine sauce equally around each serving.

Roasted Scottish Grouse, Speck, Young Onions, and Chanterelle Sauce

For hunters, the grouse is a difficult target; for foodies, it's a heavenly treat. The season opens on August 12, known in England and Scotland as "The Glorious Twelfth." Following this illustrious tradition, I eat roasted grouse every August.

SERVES 4

4 grouse

4 small pears

¼ cup (50 mL) vinegar

½ cup (125 mL) sugar

1 cup (250 mL) butter, approx.
  (separated into ¼ cups/50 mL)

5 oz (150 g) chanterelle mushrooms

5 oz (150 g) young onions

1 cup (250 mL) red wine

½ cup (125 mL) duck jus (see p. 219)

4 oz (120 g) speck (or lightly smoked bacon),
  julienned

Preheat the oven to 350°F (180°C).

Rub the grouse with butter. Season generously with salt and pepper and sear on all sides until bronzed. Then roast the grouse in the oven for 25 minutes. To poach the pears, bring a saucepan of water (enough to cover the pears) to a boil, add the vinegar and sugar, and stir until the sugar has completely dissolved. Reduce the heat and poach the pears for 10 to 15 minutes, until they are tender but not falling apart.

Warm ¼ cup (50 mL) of the butter in a small cast-iron or nonstick pan and roast the pears, mushrooms, onions, and speck together over low heat for approximately 10 minutes, adding up to ½ cup (125 mL) more butter as required until the pears start to caramelize.

Remove the grouse to a platter and deglaze the roasting pan with the red wine, stirring to scrape up the brown bits from the bottom and sides of the pan. Stir in the duck jus and pour the liquid through a fine sieve into a saucepan. Add the speck and reduce by two-thirds. Whisk in the remaining ¼ cup (50 mL) butter.

Arrange the grouse on 4 plates with a pear and a serving of chanterelles and young onions. Generously spoon the red wine reduction over the top.

Sockeye Salmon Tournedos and Warm Summer Vegetable and Mint Salad with Heirloom Tomato Nage

This dish is a kaleidoscope of colours, from red to bright orange, green to golden yellow. Keep the colours flowing by serving a chilled rosé from Provence to cool on a hot summer night.

SERVES 4

24 oz (675 g) raw sockeye salmon fillet, skinned
2 tbsp (30 mL) butter
Salt and pepper to taste
4 baby fennel, cut in half lengthwise
4 baby turnips, cut in half lengthwise
1 cup (250 mL) chopped heirloom carrots

1 cup (250 mL) chopped zucchini
½ cup (125 mL) celery leaves
½ cup (125 mL) olive oil
2 tbsp (30 mL) lemon juice
1–2 mint leaves, chopped
2 cups (500 mL) tomato consommé (see p. 220)

Trim the fattest part of belly and then cut the salmon into thin 3-inch (8 cm) long strips crosswise. Butter a 3-inch (8 cm) wide spot on each heat-proof serving plate, season the butter, and arrange the strips of salmon in a circular shape to form a medallion (you'll need 2 to 3 strips per serving). Torch about 10 seconds per side (the salmon must remain rare) and set aside.

Prepare and cook the fennel, turnips, carrots, zucchini, and celery leaves according to your preference, then toss in the olive oil, lemon juice, and mint leaves.

In 4 bowls, arrange the warm vegetable salad around the salmon medallions. Top each serving with ½ cup (125 mL) tomato consommé.

NOTE: The quantities of vegetables are meant only as a guide—simply use as much or as little of each as you prefer.

We pride ourselves on our brioche and, more often than not, sell out of them early in the morning. As a result, my kids seldom get to enjoy this dessert. Thankfully, they're not yet old enough to know the cruelty of this small injustice.

SERVES 4

ROASTED FRUIT

1 tbsp (15 mL) unsalted butter

2 tbsp (30 mL) sugar

1 cup (250 mL) raspberries

1 cup (250 mL) halved strawberries

1 cup (250 mL) cherries, pitted

1 peach, sliced

½ cup (125 mL) red currants

VANILLA BASIL ICE CREAM

1²/₃ cups (400 mL) milk

1²/₃ cups (400 mL) whipping cream

2 vanilla beans, halved and scraped

1 bunch basil

¾ cup (175 mL) sugar

7 egg yolks

1 tbsp (15 mL) pastis

FRENCH TOAST

3 large eggs

2 large egg yolks

½ cup (125 mL) sugar

1 vanilla bean, halved and scraped

½ cup (125 mL) milk

½ cup (125 mL) whipping cream

4 slices of brioche loaf, cut
    ¾ inch (2 cm) thick

1 cup (125 mL) icing sugar

6 tbsp (90 mL) unsalted butter

ROASTED BERRIES

Melt the butter in a large skillet over medium heat. Add the sugar and dissolve for 1 to 2 minutes. Carefully stir in the berries. Reduce the liquid by half, remove from heat, and set aside.

ICE CREAM

In a saucepan, bring the milk, cream, and vanilla seeds to a simmer. Remove from the heat, stir in the basil, and cover with plastic wrap. Infuse for 20 minutes, then strain to remove the basil and vanilla seeds.

Meanwhile, in a large bowl, whisk the sugar with the yolks until doubled in volume. Transfer to a saucepan over low heat and pour in the warm infused milk. Allow to thicken, stirring constantly with a wooden spoon. Mix in the pastis.

Chill over ice and then pour into an ice-cream maker and churn until smooth and thick, according to the manufacturer's instructions. Place in the freezer for at least 1 hour.

FRENCH TOAST

In a mixing bowl, beat together the eggs, egg yolks, and sugar. Add the vanilla seeds, milk, and cream, stirring until blended.

Soak each slice of brioche thoroughly in the egg mixture and place on a platter. Using a fine sieve, sift ¼ cup (50 mL) of the icing sugar over the soaked brioche, making sure it's evenly covered on one side.

Melt the butter in a large skillet over medium heat. Add the brioche slices, sugared side down, and cook for 4 to 6 minutes or until lightly browned on the bottom. Flip and sift ¼ cup (50 mL) of the icing sugar over the tops. Cook until lightly browned, adding more butter if necessary.

Spoon the roasted berries over the French toast, top with the vanilla basil ice cream, and dust with the remaining icing sugar.

Raspberry Gâteau with Lavender-Infused Crème Anglaise

When I lived in Europe, I used a lot of lavender—this wonderfully fragrant herb covers the countryside in the south of France. When I moved to Canada, I bought a farm with lavender growing on the pasture all around the house, so it's always been part of my cooking.

SERVES 4

LAVENDER-INFUSED CRÈME ANGLAISE
1 cup (250 mL) whipping cream
1 vanilla bean, split and scraped
4 sprigs lavender
3 egg yolks
⅓ cup (75 mL) sugar

SEL DE GUÉRANDE NOUGATINE
⅓ cup (75 mL) sugar
3 tbsp (45 mL) glucose
4 tsp (20 mL) sliced almonds
4 tsp (20 mL) sesame seeds
1 tsp (5 mL) sel de Guérande

RASPBERRY GÂTEAU
¼ cup (50 mL) butter
1½ cups (375 mL) sugar
2 tbsp (30 mL) grated orange zest
8 egg yolks
7 tbsp (105 mL) all-purpose flour
¼ cup (50 mL) freshly squeezed orange juice
2 cups (500 mL) milk
6 egg whites
4 cups (1 L) raspberries

Preheat the oven to 300°F (150°C).

LAVENDER-INFUSED CRÈME ANGLAISE
Combine the cream, vanilla seeds, and lavender sprigs in a saucepan over medium heat. Bring to a simmer. In a bowl, whisk the egg yolks with the sugar. Pour the cream mixture a little at a time into the eggs and sugar while whisking. Return to the saucepan and to medium heat, stirring continuously with a wooden spoon in a figure-eight pattern until the mixture coats the back of the spoon.

Remove from the heat and cool in the fridge. Immediately before serving, blend until frothy with a hand blender and pass though a fine sieve.

SEL DE GUÉRANDE NOUGATINE
Make a caramel by cooking the sugar and glucose in a skillet or copper sugar pot. When it reaches the desired caramel colour, add the almonds and sesame seeds, working well with a wooden spoon. Stir in the sel de Guérande.

Pour onto a baking sheet lined with parchment paper. Roll out with a greased rolling pin and allow to cool. Place another parchment paper on top and crack with a wooden mallet until you obtain nougatine cracklings.

RASPBERRY GÂTEAU

In a food processor, cream the butter, sugar, and orange zest. Add the yolks one at a time and mix. Add the flour and pulse. Lastly, pour in the orange juice and milk and mix.

In a separate bowl, beat the egg whites until stiff peaks form and fold into the batter. Pour the batter into a Pyrex or other oven-proof dish lined with plastic wrap and place in a double boiler in the preheated oven. Bake about 30 minutes, until golden brown and firm. Allow to cool, then carefully unmould on a baking sheet. Place in the fridge overnight.

Using a square cookie cutter, cut out 4 small gâteaux. Place each in the centre of 4 plates. Arrange the raspberries on top of the gâteaux, drizzle the lavender-infused crème anglaise around the plates, and sprinkle with sel de Guérande nougatine.

Strawberry Gratin with Wild Peppermint

After picking your own strawberries, this is a perfect recipe to enjoy with your family. I have to thank my old friend and colleague François Kovalski, who never objects to driving from his home in Labrador just to bring me some fresh wild peppermint.

SERVES 4

6 egg yolks
¾ cup (175 mL) sugar
5 tbsp (75 mL) kirsch
1 vanilla bean, split
2 lb (1 kg) strawberries, cleaned and hulled
1 tbsp (15 mL) chopped wild (or cultivated) peppermint

Combine the egg yolks, ¼ cup (50 mL) of the sugar, 4 tbsp (60 mL) of the kirsch, and the seeds from the vanilla bean in a heat-proof bowl. Place the bowl on top of a saucepan of simmering water, making sure the bottom of the bowl doesn't touch the water. Whisk until the mixture doubles in volume and becomes thick and pale. Set aside.

In a mixing bowl, toss the strawberries, remaining sugar, kirsch, and wild peppermint. Divide among 4 oven-safe ramekins. Pour the egg yolk mixture on top and place under a broiler until golden brown.

Verrine of Strawberry, White Chocolate, and Coconut-Flavoured Lemon Verbena

My favourite summer fruit "martini," smooth and sweet.

5 oz (150 g) white chocolate
¾ cup (175 mL) warm milk
2 gelatin sheets, soaked in warm water
½ cup (125 mL) strawberries, washed and hulled
½ cup (125 mL) sugar
2 tsp (10 mL) lemon juice
2 tbsp (30 mL) finely grated fresh coconut
6 whole strawberries
6 lemon verbena leaves

Melt the white chocolate over a double boiler. Add the warm milk and previously soaked gelatin sheets. Whisk until smooth and set aside to cool a little until the mixture starts to thicken slightly. Cool to room temperature.

In a mixing bowl, combine the hulled strawberries, 3 tbsp (45 mL) of the sugar, and the lemon juice. Mash together with a fork. In a separate bowl, mix the remaining sugar with the coconut and set aside.

Divide the strawberry mixture among 6 large martini glasses. Pour the white chocolate mixture carefully on top of the strawberries. Place in the fridge for 4 hours until firm. Before serving, garnish with a whole strawberry and a lemon verbena leaf dipped in the coconut mixture.

My Asian-Style Beef Ribs

This is my wife Biana's favourite summer barbecue meal. Clearly, it had to make the cut in my cookbook, or I wouldn't be here telling you this story.

SERVES 4

¼ cup (50 mL) rice wine vinegar
2 tbsp (30 mL) chopped garlic
2 tbsp (30 mL) chopped coriander
1 tbsp (15 mL) chopped gingerroot
6 fresh kaffir lime leaves
½ cup (125 mL) teriyaki sauce
½ cup (125 mL) hoisin sauce
¼ cup (50 mL) honey
4 lb (2 kg) beef back ribs
Sea salt to taste
1 tsp (5 mL) freshly ground Szechuan peppercorns

Preheat one side of the barbecue to 250°F (120°C).

In a blender or a food processor, blend the rice wine vinegar, garlic, coriander, gingerroot, and lime leaves. Blend in the teriyaki sauce, then the hoisin, and finally the honey. Set aside.

Trim excess fat from the ribs. Rub with sea salt and Szechuan peppercorns. Place the ribs on the cool side of the grill and close the lid. Slow-cook for 2½ to 3 hours, or until the meat is tender. During the last 15 minutes, baste with the Asian-style sauce until you achieve a thick coating.

Immediately before serving, brush with sauce to glaze thoroughly.

FALL

There's something a little bit sad about the start of fall, when the sunshine goes away and the rains come—but then that makes me happy, too, because it means it's time to dust off my guns and head to the woods and the wetlands. I love pheasant and especially woodcock, which is great for terrines. My favourite is duck, which is totally different when it's wild—it has much more flavour, but it's also a little tough, so I cook it really, really slowly, wrapped in bacon, basted again and again, and serve it with sauerkraut—which is what you have to do when you come from Alsace.

The duck also goes really well with a sauce I make with white grapes, and those are at their best in the fall—when their acidity and sweetness are in perfect balance. Same thing with apples and wild blueberries. And that's good, because my kids don't hunt yet, so I take them fruit picking instead.

In France—and I guess it's the same in England, and Germany, all over Europe—fall is traditionally the time for killing your pigs, which are fat from foraging all summer and ready to be turned into things you can eat for the rest of the year. Boudin for right away, hams for Christmas, cured sausages for later in the year, prosciutto a year after that. I don't keep pigs anymore, but I still get in the mood to make a lot of sausages in the fall.

Fall vegetables have so much flavour. There's cabbage for sauerkraut, and I like squash just as much. We have such good varieties here that I hadn't used in France, like the butternut, which is so rich and good for soups and raviolis. The most surprising squash I tried here was the one that's so important to the biggest feast of the season: the pumpkin, in a warm, spicy pumpkin pie.

BREAKFAST

White Truffle Scrambled Eggs 118

Milk Jam with Sourdough Baguette 120

LUNCH APPETIZER

Salad of Duck Confit and Puy Lentils with White Truffle Vinaigrette 121

Oven-Dried Heirloom Tomato Brochette with Mozzarella and Radicchio on a
Garlic Baguette with Roasted Peppers 122

LUNCH SANDWICH

Duck Club with Maple-Cured Bacon, Smoked Tomato Relish, and Douanier Cheese 125

LUNCH MAIN COURSE

Porcini Mushroom Risotto 126

Sweetbread Casserole with Hedgehog Mushrooms, Bacon, Grapes, and Pinot Noir 128

Beer-Brined Organic Chicken with Grape, Arugula, and Sourdough Salad with
Aged Xérès Vinaigrette 130

Confit of Arctic Char with Roasted Tomatoes, Red Wine–Poached Eggs, and Verjus Emulsion 131

DINNER APPETIZER

Roasted Pumpkin Soup with Poached Bone Marrow and White Truffle 134

Duck Carpaccio with Pear Brunoise, Stuffed Dates, Toasted Sumac Seeds,
and White Truffle Vinaigrette 136

Quail Consommé with Poached Foie Gras, Pine Mushrooms, and Quail Aiguillettes 138

Oyster Froth with Caviar and Pickled Strawberry Brunoise 139

DINNER MAIN COURSE

DESSERT

THANKSGIVING DINNER

PANTRY

White Truffle Scrambled Eggs

Quite simply, this is as close to a food orgasm as you can get. Don't believe me? Experience the excitement yourself.

8 free-range eggs
7 tsp (35 mL) whipping cream
7 tsp (35 mL) unsalted butter
2½ oz (75 g) fresh white truffle, chopped
1 tsp (5 mL) chopped chives

In a bowl, whisk the eggs and whipping cream very gently together. Heat a pan over high heat and add the butter. When the butter starts to foam, take off the heat and pour in the egg mixture. Return to the heat and stir with a wooden spoon. Add the white truffle and chives and mix for another minute or so until scrambled.

Scoop the scrambled egg into an egg cup or the hollowed eggshell. Top with 2 shavings of white truffle.

NOTE: To increase their flavour before using, store the truffles in a jar with 4 oiled eggs resting on paper towels for 4 to 5 days. The longer they're jarred, the better the flavour. If you'd like to present this dish in a different way, serve the scrambled eggs in the eggshell on top of black Hawaiian sea salt. Crack the eggs with an egg topper to ensure a clean cut. Put the eggs in a bowl and carefully clean out the shells.

Our bakery is an integral part of our business, and our hand-rolled baguette, which we call La Retro, is by far the most popular item in our stores. Topped with this special jam it's a great way to start the day.

SERVES 4

8 cups (2 L) whole milk
2 cups (500 mL) sugar
Pinch of baking soda
1 sourdough baguette

Preheat the oven to 300°F (150°C).

In a heavy copper pot, bring the milk to a simmer. Add the sugar and baking soda, stirring with a wooden spoon until combined. Reduce the heat to allow the mixture to simmer gently. Cook, stirring often, until the mixture thickens, about 45 minutes. After thickening, continue to stir until the mixture turns golden brown, making sure the milk doesn't burn. If the mixture becomes too dark, immediately take off the heat for a few minutes.

Remove from the heat and divide among warm, sterilized Mason jars. Seal the jars and refrigerate (sealed jars will keep in the fridge for up to 2 months).

Slice the baguette in half lengthwise. Cut the two lengthwise pieces into thirds. Bake for 2 minutes. Spread milk jam on the baguette pieces and serve.

This dish is a fine combination of luxury and simplicity.

SERVES 4

PUY LENTILS
18 oz (500 g) Puy lentils
1 onion, peeled and studded with 3 cloves
2 cups (250 mL) diced carrots
Salt to taste
1 tsp (5 mL) chopped shallots
1 tbsp (15 mL) chopped chives
⅓ cup (75 mL) white truffle vinaigrette (see p. 227)

DUCK CONFIT
4 duck legs (canard gras)
Sea salt to taste
1 garlic clove, halved
1 sprig rosemary
4 cups (1 L) duck fat
Sliced white truffle to garnish (optional)

Soak the lentils in cold water for at least 3 hours and drain. Place in a large pot and cover with cold water. Add the onion and carrots and bring to a simmer. While simmering, carefully skim the impurities from the top with a ladle.

After 15 minutes, season with salt and cook for another 20 minutes or until cooked. To test for doneness, squeeze a lentil between two fingers; if cooked, the lentil will break. Strain and set aside.

To make the duck confit, heavily season the duck legs with sea salt. Place in a Pyrex dish and add the garlic and rosemary. Cover and refrigerate for 24 hours.

Remove the duck legs and rinse under cold running water, making sure all the salt is removed. Pat dry.

In a heavy saucepan, heat the duck fat to 160°F (70°C). Carefully place the duck legs in the fat and slow-cook on the stovetop or in the oven for at least 2 hours. Use a thermometer to maintain a steady temperature of 160° (70°C). After 2 hours, use a skewer to test whether the duck is cooked. The skewer should go through the duck leg without resistance. Remove the legs from the fat and set aside to cool.

In a nonstick pan on medium heat, sear the duck legs skin side down. Cover. When the skin is golden brown, pour out the excess fat and turn the legs over. Cook 5 minutes longer or until hot and crisp-skinned.

Mix the lentils with the shallots and chives. Stir in the white truffle vinaigrette and season to taste. Divide the lentils among 4 plates. Place the hot duck legs on top and garnish with slices of white truffle, if desired.

Oven-Dried Heirloom Tomato Brochette with Mozzarella and Radicchio on a Garlic Baguette with Roasted Peppers

In mid-fall the heirloom tomato makes its last appearance. Here's a great way to bid goodbye to this wonderful fruit.

SERVES 4

OVEN-DRIED TOMATOES

4 heirloom tomatoes, red and yellow

4 tbsp (60 mL) olive oil

2 garlic cloves, minced

2 tbsp (30 mL) finely chopped fresh basil

2 tbsp (30 mL) finely chopped thyme

Salt and pepper to taste

PEPPERS, BAGUETTE, AND SALAD

2 peppers, red and yellow

4 tbsp (60 mL) olive oil

1 baguette, sliced

3 tbsp (45 mL) unsalted butter

2 garlic cloves, minced

4 buffalo mozzarella balls

Radicchio and romaine lettuce, roughly chopped

8 black olives

To make the oven-dried tomatoes, cut the tomatoes into ½-inch (1 cm) slices. In a bowl, toss with the olive oil, garlic, basil, thyme, salt, and pepper. Spread in a single layer on a parchment paper–lined baking sheet and roast overnight in a 100°F (35°C) oven.

Toss the peppers with the olive oil and roast on a tray in a 300°F (150°C) oven for approximately 40 minutes, turning once during this time. Remove, place in a bowl, and cover with plastic wrap. When cooled, peel and quarter.

Cut the baguette into ¼-inch (5 mm) slices, on a bias. Melt the butter in a frying pan over medium-high heat. Fry the baguette slices with the garlic for 2 to 3 minutes per side until golden brown and crisp.

Cut the buffalo mozzarella balls into 4 to 6 slices each. Layer the oven-dried tomato and cheese slices on top of each other to make 4 stacks, placing a skewer through them, if necessary, to hold them together.

Arrange the radicchio and romaine in the centre of 4 plates. Place the tomato and cheese skewers on top of the lettuce, and fan the baguette around the edge of the plates. Garnish with 2 quartered roasted peppers and 2 whole black olives per plate.

Duck Club with Maple-Cured
Bacon, Smoked Tomato Relish
and Douanier Cheese

I love duck. The nicest lunch for me is a great club sandwich made with duck meat.

SERVES 4

SMOKED TOMATO RELISH

12 Roma tomatoes, blanched
    and peeled

1 sweet onion, halved

2 garlic cloves

4 tbsp (60 mL) grapeseed oil

1 sprig thyme

¼ tsp (1 mL) salt

¼ tsp (1 mL) pepper

2 tbsp (30 mL) olive oil

OVEN-ROASTED TOMATOES

1 heirloom tomato

2 tbsp (30 mL) olive oil

1 garlic clove, chopped

1 tsp (5 mL) chopped fresh thyme

2 tbsp (30 mL) chopped fresh basil

Salt and pepper to taste

DUCK CLUB

1 duck breast

2 tbsp (30 mL) olive oil

4 slices foie gras

4 rashers maple-cured bacon

1 tbsp (15 mL) grapeseed oil

4 circles milk bread (pain au lait)

Romaine, or any crisp lettuce

4 thin slices Douanier (or Reblochon
    or Morbier) cheese

For the tomato relish, prepare a stove-top smoker with 2 tbsp (30 mL) of smoking chips on the very bottom. Place the whole tomatoes, onion (cut side down), and garlic on the rack inside the smoker. Smoke on high heat for 5 to 7 minutes. Let cool for 10 minutes with the lid closed. Once cool, roughly chop the tomatoes, julienne the onion, and mince the garlic. Heat the grapeseed oil in a saucepan over medium-high heat. Add the sliced onion and thyme, sautéing until the onions are translucent. Stir in the garlic and chopped tomato, as well as salt and pepper. Cook for about 10 minutes, stirring often. Remove the thyme and mix in the olive oil. Serve at room temperature.

To oven-roast the tomatoes, cut the tomato into ½-inch (1 cm) slices. In a bowl, toss with the olive oil, garlic, thyme, basil, salt, and pepper. Spread in a single layer on a parchment paper–lined baking sheet and roast in a 100°F (35°C) oven overnight.

To finish the club sandwich, score the fat on the one side of the duck breast. Heat the olive oil in a pan over high heat and sear the duck, starting skin side down, for about 3 to 4 minutes per side until medium-rare. Slice thinly.

Heat a pan over high heat and sear the foie gras for 1 minute per side until golden brown. Pan-fry the bacon in the grapeseed oil until crispy and drain on paper towels.

Lightly toast the bread rounds. Layer each piece with the smoked tomato relish, then a leaf of romaine, a slice of bacon, a roasted tomato, a slice of Douanier cheese, and the duck breast. Season and sear the foie gras for about 1 minute per side and place on top. Serve at once.

Porcini Mushroom Risotto

Thank you, Franco Prevedello, for teaching me the traditional way of making a great risotto. Thankfully, mother nature provided porcini mushrooms to make this risotto taste even better.

SERVES 4

2 tbsp (30 mL) olive oil
3 shallots, chopped
1 garlic clove, chopped
1 cup (250 mL) sliced porcini mushrooms
1¼ cups (300 mL) arborio rice
²/₃ cup (150 mL) dry white wine
8 cups (2 L) chicken stock (see p. 215)
¼ cup (50 mL) butter
2 tbsp (30 mL) mascarpone
1 cup (250 mL) grated Parmigiano-Reggiano cheese
Fleur de sel and white pepper to taste

Heat the olive oil in a heavy-bottomed pot. Sauté the shallots and garlic until translucent. Stir in the mushrooms and cook until light brown.

Add the rice and stir with a wooden spoon for 2 minutes. Pour in the white wine and reduce for 2 minutes. Add 5 ladles of chicken stock and bring to a simmer while stirring constantly. Lower the heat. When the rice has absorbed all the liquid, ladle in more chicken stock. Repeat until the rice is cooked to al dente, approximately 20 minutes.

Stir in the butter, the mascarpone, and half the grated Parmesan. Season to taste with fleur de sel and white pepper. Add a final ladle of chicken stock, cooking 2 minutes longer on very low heat until the risotto is creamy.

Divide among 4 plates and sprinkle with the remaining grated Parmesan. I like to finish with a little fleur de sel on top for crunch.

Sweetbread Casserole with Hedgehog Mushrooms, Bacon, Grapes, and Pinot Noir

This dish pairs a few of my favourite Canadian ingredients with some of the most beloved French delicacies.

SERVES 4

CASSEROLE
4 tbsp (60 mL) butter
1 tbsp (15 mL) sugar
3 oz (90 g) pearl onions, peeled
2 cups (500 mL) water
3 oz (90 g) hedgehog mushrooms
7 oz (200 g) sweetbreads
3 oz (90 g) bacon

PINOT NOIR REDUCTION
1 shallot, diced
3 tbsp (45 mL) Pinot Noir
½ cup (125 mL) veal jus (see p. 223)
1 tbsp (15 mL) cold butter, cubed
16 grapes, skinned

Set a pan over medium heat and add 2 tbsp (30 mL) of the butter and the sugar. Stir in the onions and sauté for 2 minutes until some colour starts to show. Pour in the water, stirring gently. Cover the pan with a parchment paper circle with a hole cut out of the middle. Cook until caramelized, about 15 minutes over low heat, adding more water if necessary to prevent the pan from burning.

In another pan, heat 1 tbsp (15 mL) of the butter over medium-high heat. Sauté the mushrooms until golden and tender, about 7 to 10 minutes.

In a third pan, sauté the sweetbreads with the remaining tablespoon of butter for about 3 to 4 minutes. Stir in the onions and mushrooms and cook for 2 minutes. Add the bacon and sauté until crisp.

For the Pinot Noir reduction, heat a touch of butter in a saucepan over high heat. Sauté the shallots for 2 minutes, and deglaze with the wine. Add the jus. Turn the heat down to medium and continue to cook for another minute. Whisk in the cold butter. Add the skinned grapes.

Spoon the sweetbread, onion, mushroom, and bacon mixture into a small dish. Top with the Pinot Noir reduction and grapes.

NOTE: Hedgehog mushrooms are a wild variety found in the forests of North America and Europe. If they're out of season, chanterelles may be substituted.

Beer-Brined Organic Chicken with Grape, Arugula, and Sourdough Salad with Aged Xérès Vinaigrette

The first time I tasted the Chantecler chicken from the Oka region in Quebec, the flavour reminded me of the type of poultry my grandmother used to raise. Unlike the bland, white meat we so often associate with poultry, this exclusive Canadian breed has a characteristic gaminess. You can certainly replace the Chantecler chicken with the organic breed from your own region.

SERVES 4

BEER-BRINED CHICKEN

12 cups (3 L) water
1 bottle Creemore Springs (or other
    quality) lager
½ cup (125 mL) brown sugar
½ cup (125 mL) white sugar
½ cup (125 mL) kosher salt
2 tbsp (30 mL) black pepper
4 tsp (20 mL) chopped gingerroot
1 tsp (5 mL) allspice
1 2-lb (1 kg) Chantecler (or other
    premium) chicken
1 tbsp (15 mL) olive oil

AGED XÉRÈS VINAIGRETTE

4 tbsp (60 mL) 20-year-old Xérès vinegar
12 tbsp (180 mL) grapeseed oil
2 tsp (10 mL) Dijon mustard
Salt and pepper to taste

SOURDOUGH CROUTONS

4 tbsp (60 mL) unsalted butter
½ cup (125 mL) sourdough bread,
    cut in 1-inch (2 cm) cubes
2 garlic cloves, finely chopped

SALAD

4 cups (1 L) arugula
1 heirloom tomato, seeded and diced
½ red onion, thinly sliced
8 halved grapes, green and black

Preheat the oven to 350°F (180°C).

To brine the chicken, bring the water to a boil in a large pot. Stir in the beer, brown sugar, white sugar, salt, pepper, gingerroot, and allspice and remove from heat. Let cool completely. Add the chicken and leave for 24 hours in the fridge.

After it has brined for a day, truss the chicken. Place in a roasting pan and brush with olive oil. Roast in the oven for 50 minutes or until a thermometer reads 160°F (70°C), turning every 10 minutes and adding more oil if necessary. When browned, remove from oven and let rest. Place on a work surface and tent with foil. While it rests, the internal temperature should rise about 10 degrees.

To make the dressing, combine the Xérès vinegar, grapeseed oil, Dijon mustard, salt, and pepper, and whisk well.

Meanwhile, heat the butter in a pan over high heat. Add the bread cubes and garlic. Sauté for about 5 minutes until crisp and golden brown.

Divide the chicken into 4 portions. In a bowl, combine the arugula, tomato, red onion, grapes, and bread cubes. Toss with vinaigrette. Serve with the chicken.

NOTE. Xérès vinegar is a rich, nutty sherry vinegar from the south of Spain. Regular sherry vinegar can be substituted.

Confit of Arctic Char with Roasted Tomatoes, Red Wine–Poached Eggs, and Verjus Emulsion

Icy Waters Arctic char is a perfect gift from Yukon, Canada. When I worked in the Alpine region in France, the chefs were also very proud of their omble chevalier, considered a prized seafood.

SERVES 4

ROASTED TOMATOES
4 heirloom tomatoes
4 tbsp (60 mL) olive oil
2 garlic cloves, finely chopped
2 tbsp (30 mL) finely chopped thyme
Salt and pepper to taste

ARCTIC CHAR
3 cups (750 mL) duck fat
4 Arctic char fillets

POACHED EGGS
2 cups (500 mL) red wine
½ cup (125 mL) red wine vinegar
4 free-range eggs

VERJUS EMULSION
4 tsp (20 mL) butter
½ cup (125 mL) verjus

To make the roasted tomatoes, cut the tomatoes into ½-inch (1 cm) slices. In a bowl, toss with the olive oil, garlic, thyme, salt, and pepper. Spread in a single layer on a parchment paper–lined baking sheet and roast overnight in a 100°F (35°C) oven.

To confit the Arctic char, heat the duck fat in a large pot over medium heat to 150°F (65°C). Add the char and cook on low heat for approximately 10 minutes, turning once. Remove from fat and take off the skin.

Combine the red wine and red wine vinegar and bring to a simmer. Crack in the eggs. Poach for about 2 minutes. The eggs will increase in size.

Add the butter to the verjus over low heat and whisk to emulsify.

Arrange 4 tomato slices on each plate and top with the confit of Arctic char. Place the poached eggs on the fillets. Drizzle with the verjus emulsion.

NOTE: Verjus is the juice from unripened green grapes that have been processed without being allowed to ferment, so there's no alcohol content. It can be purchased in most fine food stores.

This soup is an ideally rich and hearty first course for when the days start getting shorter and cooler.

SERVES 6

6 cups (1.5 L) roasted sweet pumpkin

1 cup (250 mL) canola oil

6 10-oz (300 g) beef marrow bones

2 tbsp (30 mL) grapeseed oil

1 large white onion, chopped

¼ cup (60 mL) maple sugar

½ tsp (2 mL) cinnamon

3 quarts (3 L) white chicken stock (see p. 215)

1 cup (250 mL) whipping cream

½ cup (125 mL) butter

¼ cup (60 mL) maple syrup

Julienned squash, julienned carrot, toasted pumpkin seeds, and white truffle shavings to garnish

Preheat the oven to 350°F (180°C).

Soak the marrow bones in lukewarm water for 24 hours, changing the water at least 4 times. Dry the bones with a cloth and stand them in a roasting tray. Bake for 15 to 20 minutes or until a skewer passes through the marrow with no resistance. Set aside.

Push out the marrow from the middle of the beef bones and set aside. Scrape the bones with a knife to rid them of any excess meat. Bring a pot of salted water to a boil, and boil the bones for 3 to 5 minutes until clean and white. Dry them thoroughly and scrape again with a knife to ensure that they're perfectly clean.

For the soup, heat the grapeseed oil in a large pot over medium-high heat and add the onion. Cook for 3 minutes until the onion is translucent. Stir in the roasted pumpkin and cook for another minute. Add the maple sugar and cinnamon, mixing well. Pour in 6 cups (1.5 L) of the chicken stock and cream. Transfer to a food processor and process until smooth. Pour back into the pot and whisk in the butter. At this point, adjust the consistency with up to 2 cups (.5 L) more stock. Strain through a fine sieve.

Bring the remaining 4 cups (1 L) of chicken stock to a simmer and add the marrow. Poach, covered, for 4 to 5 minutes until soft all the way through. Cut the marrow in half.

Place the bones in the centre of a bowl. Pour in the soup and place the two halves of bone marrow on top of the bones. Garnish with julienned squash and carrot; sprinkle with 3 toasted pumpkin seeds and white truffle shavings. Drizzle with maple syrup.

Duck Carpaccio with Pear Brunoise, Stuffed Dates, Toasted Sumac Seeds, and White Truffle Vinaigrette

Duck has such an elegant flavour. This dish is one of my favourites.

SERVES 4

4 oz (120 g) duck breast, skin removed, fat trimmed
1 Bartlett pear
1 (preferably Hungarian blue) plum
1 fig, skin removed
2 Medjool dates
4 tsp (20 mL) Dragon's Breath (or other blue, cow's milk quality) cheese

20 sumac seeds
Frisée
2 tbsp (30 mL) white truffle vinaigrette (see p. 227)
Sliced pickled black radish, julienned endive, cloudberry purée, and sesame oil to garnish

Cut the duck into 12 thin slices. Finely slice the pear and plum. Cut 4 slices of fig and remove the skin, so you have 4 fig wheels. Cut the dates in half lengthwise and remove the pits. Fill the 4 halves of dates with Dragon's Breath cheese.

Toast the sumac seeds in a small skillet over medium heat, or place them under the broiler for 10 seconds.

Lay the duck slices in the middle of a serving plate, slightly overlapping them. Fan out the pear and plum slices around the duck. Arrange the frisée, fig wheels, and dates studded with cheese on the plate. Sprinkle with sumac seeds and drizzle with truffle vinaigrette.

Garnish with a slice of pickled black radish, julienned endive, cloudberry purée, and a small drizzle of sesame oil.

NOTE: Pickled black radish and cloudberry purée are available at fine food stores. Dragon's Breath is a blue cheese made in Nova Scotia. As it's licensed for sale only in Nova Scotia, it can't be resold outside the province. However, it can be purchased online year-round. As a substitute, Roquefort, Rassembleu, or Stilton may be used.

Quail Consommé with Poached Foie Gras, Pine Mushrooms, and Quail Aiguillettes

A few years ago I went to Tofino, B.C., where we picked baskets full of intensely perfumed pine mushrooms, also known as matsutake. It's one of the greatest mushrooms, but I'd still rather go truffle hunting and let the dogs do the work.

SERVES 4

QUAIL STOCK
4 quails
¼ cup (50 mL) olive oil
1 onion, roughly chopped
1 carrot, roughly chopped
½ cup (125 mL) chopped celery root
6 juniper berries
2 bay leaves
1 sprig rosemary
12 cups (3 L) cold water

CONSOMMÉ
4 egg whites, yolks reserved
½ lb (250 g) ground chicken breast
1 tomato, seeded and chopped
2 tsp (10 mL) salt
1 tsp (5 mL) black peppercorns
3 juniper berries
1 bay leaf
1 sprig rosemary
1 sprig thyme

PRESENTATION
2 quail breasts, thinly sliced
4 pine mushrooms
4 quail egg yolks
4 slices foie gras

Preheat the oven to 350°F (180°C).

To make the stock, remove the legs and breast from the quail, keeping the legs for another use and setting aside 2 breasts to finish the soup. Roast the quail carcasses in the oven until browned, about 10 minutes. Heat the oil in a large pot over medium-high. Add onion, carrot, celery root, juniper berries, bay leaves, rosemary, and roasted bones. Sauté for 1 minute.

Cover with water and bring to a boil. Turn the heat down and simmer, uncovered, for 3 hours. During this time, continually skim the stock with a ladle. After 3 hours you should be left with approximately 6 cups (1.5 L). Remove from heat, discard the bay leaves and quail bones, and cool completely.

For the consommé, whisk the egg whites until foamy. In a food processor, combine the ground chicken, tomato, salt, peppercorns, juniper berries, bay leaf, rosemary, and thyme; mix well. Mix in the egg whites. Add to the stock and whisk well. Continue stirring until it begins to simmer and then stop. It is important not to stir the consommé during this time to ensure that it stays clear. Remove from heat and, with a ladle, carefully scoop out the clear stock. Strain through a fine sieve and season to taste.

When ready to plate, return the consommé to the pot and bring to a light boil. (The hot consommé will cook the quail and eggs.) Divide the sliced quail breast among 4 bowls. Place a mushroom, the quail egg yolk, and the foie gras around the quail breast. Ladle the consommé over top.

NOTE: White or black truffles can be substituted for the pine mushrooms.

Oyster Froth with Caviar and Pickled Strawberry Brunoise

This combination of oyster and caviar is a well-established classic. The addition of strawberry renders it magical.

SERVES 4

PICKLED STRAWBERRIES
1 cup (250 mL) sugar
½ cup (125 mL) rice wine vinegar
½ cup (125 mL) water
1 cinnamon stick
3 star anise
1 tsp (5 mL) Indonesian peppercorns
1 garlic clove, halved
3 kaffir lime leaves
1 cup (250 mL) hulled whole strawberries

OYSTERS
4 oysters on the shell
4 tbsp (60 mL) white wine vinegar
2 tbsp (30 mL) fish stock (see p. 216)
5 tbsp (75 mL) whipping cream
2 tbsp (30 mL) whipped cream
2 tsp (10 mL) black caviar
Julienned cucumber to garnish

Combine the sugar, rice wine vinegar, water, cinnamon stick, star anise, Indonesian peppercorns, garlic, and kaffir lime leaves in a saucepan, and bring to a boil for 5 minutes. Cool until lukewarm.

Place the strawberries in a warm, sterilized Mason jar and cover with the liquid. If you're not using them right away, store in the fridge. When you're ready to prepare this dish, take some pickled strawberries out and cut them into ⅛-inch (3 mm) cubes.

Scrub the oysters well. Shuck and reserve shells. Soak the oysters in the white wine vinegar for at least 2 hours. Place the oysters back in their shells.

Heat the fish stock in a small saucepan over medium-high heat. Stir in the cream. Heat to a near simmer, add the whipped cream, and blend with a hand blender for a few seconds to create foam.

Spoon a mound of sea salt or rice on 4 plates and perch one half of an oyster shell with the marinated oyster on top. Spoon a dollop of froth and ½ tsp (2 mL) black caviar on each serving. If desired, place the other half of the shell to the side for presentation. Garnish with julienned cucumber and pickled strawberries.

Toro Tuna Steak and Confit of Foie Gras with Teriyaki Béarnaise and Sake Emulsion

A festival of Japanese and French glorious fat.

SERVES 4

TUNA AND FOIE GRAS

4 2-oz (60 g) toro (tuna belly) fillets
Oil for searing
2 cups (500 mL) duck fat
3 oz (90 g) raw foie gras

TERIYAKI BÉARNAISE

1¼ cups (300 mL) butter
¾ cup (175 mL) rice wine vinegar
2 shallots, finely chopped
1 tbsp (15 mL) gingerroot
1 tsp (10 mL) crushed peppercorns
5 egg yolks
Salt and pepper to taste
2 tbsp (30 mL) chopped fresh tarragon
1 tbsp (15 mL) chopped fresh coriander
2 tbsp (30 mL) teriyaki sauce

SAKE EMULSION

1 shallot, finely chopped
2 garlic cloves, crushed
1 lemongrass stalk, bruised
1-inch (2.5 cm) piece gingerroot, sliced
1½ tsp (7 mL) sesame oil
¾ cup (175 mL) coconut milk
3 kaffir lime leaves
3 tbsp (45 mL) sake
2 tbsp (30 mL) rice wine vinegar
1 tbsp (15 mL) mirin (sweet cooking wine)

GARNISH

Daikon radish, cut in a brunoise
Cucumber, cut in a brunoise
Gingerroot, cut in a brunoise
Rice paper crisp

TUNA AND FOIE GRAS

Season the tuna fillets. Add the oil to a pan over high heat. Sear the tuna on all sides very quickly to brown, keeping the inside raw.

Warm the duck fat over medium heat to 150°F (65°C). Put the foie gras in the pot and reduce the heat to low. Poach for 2 to 3 minutes.

TERIYAKI BÉARNAISE

For the teriyaki béarnaise, clarify the butter by melting it in a saucepan over medium heat. Spoon off the foam as it forms and discard it. Keep skimming until the butter stops bubbling, being careful not to brown. Set aside in a warm place.

In a heavy-bottomed saucepan, heat the vinegar, shallots, gingerroot, and peppercorns over medium heat. Reduce by one-quarter. Remove from heat and pass through cheesecloth. Transfer to a heat-proof bowl and cool. Place the bowl on top of a saucepan of simmering water. Vigorously whisk the egg yolks into the vinegar mixture, making sure the temperature doesn't exceed 65°F (20°C). When the sauce reaches a creamy consistency, remove from the heat and slowly whisk in the clarified butter. Season to taste. Stir in the coriander, tarragon, and teriyaki sauce and set aside in a warm place.

SAKE EMULSION

For the sake emulsion, sweat the shallots, garlic, lemongrass, and gingerroot in a saucepan over medium heat in the sesame oil. Stir in the coconut milk and kaffir lime leaves and simmer over low heat for 5 minutes. Allow to rest for 20 minutes and strain. In another saucepan, bring the sake, rice wine vinegar, and mirin to a simmer. Pour both mixtures in a blender and emulsify.

TO FINISH

Place the tuna fillets in the middle of the plate. Roll the confit of foie gras and place it beside the tuna. Spoon the béarnaise around the tuna and drizzle with the sake emulsion. Garnish with daikon radish, cucumber, gingerroot, and a rice paper crisp.

I'd like to dedicate this recipe to my late friend and colleague, Willy Fida. We created this wonderful dish for one of our special dinners at the Châteauneuf restaurant when I first came to Canada.

SERVES 4

FOIE GRAS MOUSSE
6 oz (175 g) raw, very cold chicken breast
3 oz (90 g) very cold foie gras
1 egg white
1 cup (250 mL) whipping cream
Salt and pepper to taste
¼ bunch chives, chopped
6 tsp (30 mL) finely chopped white truffle

PIGEON SUPRÊME
4 boned pigeon breasts
8 5- by 5-inch (12 by 12 cm) sheets puff pastry
1 egg

WILD BLUEBERRY ESSENCE
½ cup (125 mL) duck jus (see p. 219)
1 tsp (5 mL) cold butter
1 tbsp (15 mL) chopped wild blueberries

Preheat the oven to 350°F (180°C).

To prepare the foie gras mousse, cut the chicken and foie gras into small cubes. It is important that they be very cold. Put into a food processor with the egg white and mix well. When smooth, add the cream and salt and pepper to taste. Pass through a fine sieve. Stir in the chives and white truffle. Divide the mixture into 4 equal portions.

In a hot pan, sear the pigeon on all sides. Lay the 8 sheets of puff pastry on your work surface. For each pigeon, spread half the portion of mousse on a sheet of pastry. Place the seared pigeon on top and cover with the remaining mousse. Cover with a second sheet of pastry. Trim the pastry to the shape of the breast. Seal the edges with a fork and score the top lightly. Beat the egg with a splash of water and brush on each pastry for colour. Bake for 40 minutes.

Meanwhile, to make the blueberry essence, heat the duck jus in a saucepan. Whisk in the cold butter until combined. Stir in the blueberries.

Place each portion of pigeon in the middle of a plate. Spoon blueberry essence on top and around the pastries.

Once in a while, a chef has the luxury of reviving some favoured recipes that defined his early career. This one comes from when I worked at the Terrace restaurant at the Dorchester and Jacques Maximin was the guest chef.

SERVES 4

8 purple figs, firm but ripe

16 thin lemon slices

2 tbsp (30 mL) olive oil

8 tsp (40 mL) butter

4 8-oz (225 g) fillets of sea bream
(preferably line-caught), skin removed

½ tbsp (7 mL) finely minced shallots

½ cup (125 mL) fish stock (see p. 216)

½ cup (125 mL) red wine

¼ cup (50 mL) port

Salt and pepper to taste

Preheat oven to 350°F (180°C).

Quarter the figs lengthwise, leaving the quarters still attached by the stem. Place 4 of the figs and 8 of the lemon slices on a baking sheet brushed with olive oil; bake for 1 hour to 1¼ hours or until firm but still moist. Set aside.

In a cast-iron skillet heat the olive oil and 1 tbsp (15 mL) of the butter over medium heat. Arrange the remaining lemon slices in the pan; top them with the remaining figs, then the sea bream. Bake until the fish becomes opaque, about 10 minutes. Remove from the oven.

Meanwhile, melt 1½ tsp (7 mL) of the butter in a saucepan and sauté the shallots until translucent. Deglaze with fish stock. Reduce by one-quarter and pour in the red wine and port. Reduce by half. Whisk in the remaining butter, adding a little at a time until incorporated. Season to taste.

Place the lemon and figs baked with the fish on 4 plates, topped with the sea bream. Garnish with the reserved lemon and fig confit. Finish with sauce.

Wild Duck with Foie Gras Canapé, Sautéed Quince, and Lingonberry-Infused Duck Jus

When this dish appears on my menu, it means summer is over—the hunting season has finally begun.

SERVES 2

1 wild duck, defeathered, innards
   removed and reserved
2 peeled quinces
6 tbsp (90 mL) butter
3 tbsp (45 mL) cognac
1 tbsp (25 mL) port
1 tbsp (30 mL) crushed juniper berries

¾ cup (200 mL) duck jus (see p. 219)
½ tbsp (7 mL) royal jelly
½ tbsp (7 mL) lingonberries
2 brioche rounds, 2 inches (5 cm) in diameter
2 tsp (10 mL) foie gras mousse (see p. 144)
Salt and pepper to taste

Preheat the oven to 375°F (190°C).

Chop the wild duck innards and one of the quinces. Melt 2 tbsp (30 mL) of the butter in a saucepan and sauté the chopped quince and duck innards for a few minutes over medium heat. Season to taste. Pour in 1 tbsp (15 mL) of the cognac and flambé. Allow to cool.

Stuff the duck with the mixture, sewing the cavity closed with a trussing needle. Place in a roasting pan and roast in the oven for approximately 30 minutes.

Meanwhile, cut the remaining peeled quince into eighths and seed. Melt 2 tbsp (30 mL) of the butter in a pan. Sauté the quince for 10 minutes or until softened. Remove from heat and set aside.

Remove the duck from the oven and place on a cutting board. Cover with foil and allow to rest.

Discard excess fat from the roasting pan. Deglaze the pan with the port and the remaining cognac. Add the crushed juniper berries. Reduce by half and stir in the duck jus. Reduce by one-quarter. Season to taste. Whisk in the remaining butter, the royal jelly, and, at the last minute, the lingonberries. Pass through a fine sieve.

Toast the brioche rounds and top with the foie gras. Place the canapés in the middle of each plate.

Carve the duck, discarding all the bones. Place a duck breast and leg on each plate. Divide the stuffing evenly and place on the plates. Arrange the sautéed quince and drizzle the plates with sauce.

NOTE: Red currants may be substituted if lingonberries are unavailable, and cultivated duck will do in a pinch.

Petite Thuet Tarte Tatin

Some people love apple pie. We love it upside down.

SERVES 8

1 cup (250 mL) unsalted butter
2 cups (500 mL) sugar
10 baking apples, peeled, halved, and cored
12-inch (30 cm) round puff pastry

Preheat the oven to 350°F (180°C).

Melt the butter and sugar in a 12-inch (30 cm) cast-iron pan. Simmer until the sugar caramelizes, turning dark golden brown, 10 to 15 minutes.

Place 12 apple halves in the caramel upright in concentric circles, packing them as tightly as possible. Place 8 halves on top of the tightly packed apples (you'll need them when the apples shrink during cooking).

Bake for 20 minutes. Remove from the oven and fill the holes with the 8 apple halves from the top. Poke the puff pastry with a fork and place on top of the apples, tucking into the edges. Cook for 20 minutes longer, or until the pastry is golden and crisp. Let cool.

To unmould, place a serving dish on top of the tarte and carefully flip over.

Serve cold or hot.

My gingerbread is guaranteed to be delicious. In this recipe, three cheeses steal the show.

GINGERBREAD TOAST

⅔ cup (150 mL) milk

¾ cup (175 mL) butter

½ cup (125 mL) organic honey

½ cup (125 mL) sugar

1 egg

¾ cup (175 mL) all-purpose flour

¾ cup (175 mL) buckwheat flour

1 tsp (5 mL) baking soda

2 tsp (10 mL) ginger

2 tsp (10 mL) cinnamon

1 tsp (5 mL) cloves

1 tsp (5 mL) ground star anise

1 tsp (5 mL) allspice

4 slices each Rassembleu,
    Mont-Jacob, and Migneron
    de Charlevoix

1 Bartlett pear, peeled, cored,
    and diced

CIDRE DE NEIGE CARAMEL

½ cup (125 mL) sugar

1 tsp (5 mL) glucose

¼ cup (50 mL) water

6½ tbsp (100 mL) cidre de Neige
    (apple ice wine)

1½ tsp (7 mL) butter

2 tsp (10 mL) fleur de sel

Preheat the oven to 350°F (180°C).

For the gingerbread toast, bring the milk to a simmer in a small saucepan.

In a heavy-bottomed pot, mix the butter, honey, and sugar. Melt together over low heat. Let cool. Add the egg and mix well.

In a mixing bowl, combine the all-purpose and buckwheat flour, baking soda, ginger, cinnamon, cloves, star anise, and allspice. Stir into the butter mixture, then add the warm milk.

Grease and flour a 10- by 5-inch (25 by 12 cm) baking sheet (it should be at least 2 inches/5 cm high). Pour in the batter. Bake for 15 to 20 minutes. Set aside to cool.

Meanwhile, to make the caramel, cook the sugar, glucose, and water in a heavy-bottomed pot until caramel coloured. Slowly stir in the cidre de Neige, adding a little at a time. Remove from heat and whisk in the butter. When the caramel is cool, sprinkle in the fleur de sel. Set aside.

With a 2½-inch (6 cm) round cookie cutter, cut rounds out of the gingerbread toast. Place a thin slice of each cheese on the rounds. Bake in a 300°F (150°C) oven for 3 minutes or until the cheese is melted.

Pour the room-temperature, salted caramel sauce in the middle of 4 plates. Place the gingerbread cheese toast on top and garnish with diced Bartlett pears.

NOTE: Rassembleu is an organic blue cheese produced in the Laurentians by Fromagerie Hamel. Mont-Jacob is a semi-soft, interior-ripened cheese from Fromagerie Blackburn in Jonquière, Quebec. Migneron de Charlevoix is a semi-soft, washed-rind cheese from Baie-Saint-Paul, Quebec. All are available at fine cheese shops. You may of course use any 3 of your preferred Canadian artisanal cheeses.

Croissant-Crust Pizza with Blood Orange Marmalade, Blue Cheese, and Black Cumin

A much easier, and certainly more fun, alternative to the typical cheese platter.

SERVES 4

4 4-inch (10 cm) rounds of croissant dough
12 Valor plums
1²/₃ cups (400 mL) vanilla-infused simple syrup
²/₃ cup (150 mL) blood orange marmalade
4 slices Dragon's Breath or other quality blue cheese
1 tsp (5 mL) black cumin

Preheat the oven to 380°F (195°C).

Bake the croissant rounds until light golden, about 5 minutes. Set aside.

Halve and pit the plums and poach for 5 minutes in the vanilla-infused simple syrup. Remove the plums and cool. Slice each half into 3 wedges.

Spread the blood orange marmalade evenly on the croissant rounds. Arrange the poached plum segments on top in a circle. Place a slice of cheese in the centre of the pizzas. Sprinkle with black cumin.

Lower the oven temperature to 350°F (175°C). Bake the pizzas for 5 minutes or until the cheese melts. Remove and serve.

NOTE: I use croissant dough for this recipe because my baker has leftover end cuts from making croissants, but you could also use puff pastry.

Simple syrup is a reduction of water and sugar. You can buy it in most fine food stores or make your own by bringing 3 parts water, 1 part sugar, and a vanilla bean to a boil. Reduce the heat to low and stir until the sugar dissolves completely.

Dragon's Breath is a blue cheese that's made in Nova Scotia and can be purchased online outside the province. Roquefort, Rassembleu, or Stilton may be substituted.

The next three dishes have become staples both at home and in my stores during Thanksgiving. This holiday is all about spending time with family, not reinventing the cooking wheel, so I like to stick to the classics. Happy Thanksgiving.

SERVES 4

⅔ cup (150 mL) butter
1 lb (500 g) parsnips, thinly sliced
1½ lb (750 g) apples, peeled, cored and sliced
1 onion, diced
⅓ cup (75 mL) brown sugar
2 tbsp (30 mL) green curry paste
2 tsp (10 mL) cinnamon
3 garlic cloves, minced
4 cups (1 L) chicken stock (see p. 215)
1¼ cups (300 mL) whipping cream
¾ cup (175 mL) whipped cream
Salt and pepper to taste

Melt half the butter in a thick-bottomed large pan over medium heat. Add the parsnips, apples, and onion and cook until soft.

Add the brown sugar, curry paste, cinnamon, and garlic, stirring continuously with a wooden spoon for 3 minutes.

Stir in the chicken stock and simmer for 20 minutes or until the parsnips are very tender. Pour in the whipping cream and simmer 10 minutes longer. Remove from heat and blend until smooth.

Reheat the soup to a light simmer. Blend in the remaining butter with a hand blender. Fold in the whipped cream, season to taste, and serve.

SERVES 6 TO 8

3 cups (750 mL) day-old sourdough
  bread, cubed and crustless
1 cup (250 mL) milk
2 onions, chopped
2 garlic cloves, minced
1 tbsp (15 mL) grapeseed oil
4½ lb (2 kg) chopped pork sausage,
  casings removed

2 eggs
2 tbsp (30 mL) fresh chopped sage
1 tbsp (15 mL) fresh chopped thyme
2 cups (500 mL) chestnut purée
1 12–16 lb (5.5–7.25 kg) heritage turkey
3 tbsp (45 mL) soft butter
Salt and pepper to taste

Preheat the oven to 400°F (200°C).

Soak the bread in the milk for 1 hour.

In a sauté pan over low heat, sweat the onions and garlic in the grapeseed oil until translucent. Do not brown. Chill.

In a stand mixer with the paddle attachment, mix the following, adding them to the bowl in order: the sausage, bread and milk, eggs, sage and thyme, sweated onion and garlic, and chestnut purée.

Stuff the mixture in the turkey cavity. Truss the turkey, massage it with soft butter, and season well.

Roast at 400°F (200°C) for 45 minutes. Then, turn the temperature down to 350°F (180°C) and cook until a meat thermometer inserted in the centre of the stuffing reaches 165°F (75°C), 2 to 2½ hours.

Remove to a cutting board, cover with foil, and let rest for 20 to 30 minutes. Carve and remove the stuffing. Serve with your favourite fall vegetables.

NOTE You'll find chestnut purée in most fine food stores.

Sweet Potato Pie

1 cup (250 mL) cooked and
    mashed sweet potatoes
1½ cups (375 mL) sugar
⅔ cup (150 mL) condensed milk
¼ cup (50 mL) softened butter
2 eggs, beaten
1 tsp (5 mL) cinnamon
1 tsp (5 mL) nutmeg
½ tsp (2 mL) ground star anise
½ tsp (2 mL) allspice
1 unbaked pie shell

Preheat the oven to 350°F (180°C).

Stir together the sweet potatoes, sugar, condensed milk, and butter in a mixing bowl. Add the eggs, cinnamon, nutmeg, star anise, and allspice, mixing well. Pour the mixture into the pie shell.

Bake for 45 minutes or until set. Cut into 8 pieces and serve with whipped cream or good-quality vanilla ice cream.

Rumtopf

For generations my family has honoured the tradition of collecting summer and fall fruit and preserving them in dark rum. In Alsace, we also call it "the celibate's jam" because of its distracting alcohol content. I can't imagine Christmas without the sweet aroma of rumtopf.

2 lb (1 kg) fruit, washed and patted dry
3 cups (750 mL) sugar
4 cups (1 L) dark rum

In a mixing bowl, combine the fruit and sugar. Set aside for 2 hours. Pour the fruit in a rumtopf (a large stoneware pot) and cover with dark rum. Set in a cool place.

Repeat these steps as new fruits come into season until the rumtopf is full.

WINTER

Smells are powerful for triggering memories, and it should be no surprise that for me, they always came from the kitchen. Or—back when I was a kid of ten or eleven—the grate in the fireplace at my uncle's house where he used to roast whole truffles. That's still the aroma of winter that I will never forget. There are lots more.

Baking is so important in Alsace that it's actually illegal for the owner of the village bakery to close it down. So when I think about winter cooking, I always think first about all the baked goods we put on the table for those two special feasts of the year—Christmas and New Year's: from basic breads like a big sourdough miche to the sweet seasonal specialties we got from each of our neighbours, bûches de Noël and stollen.

For Christmas in Alsace we don't eat turkey, we eat goose, usually a huge fat one that we roast at a low temperature for five or six hours until the fat is rendered and the skin is golden and crisp. The meal begins the same way all across France, with a boudin blanc, hopefully with truffles inside. And in my version, it ends with apple pie and ice cream *à ma façon*—a three-inch-deep pie enriched with pastry cream and almonds.

A more typical winter meal is hearty stew. My favourite is civet, a game stew of wild rabbit, the sauce thickened with its blood. Here I make it with caribou or deer and marinate the meat for days in red wine before cooking it as slowly as possible. The vegetables that last in the cold cellar—like carrots, beets, turnips, and parsnips—are all best roasted. Big flavours for cold weather, flavours that get you ready to enjoy the contrast of spring.

DINNER MAIN COURSE

DESSERT

CHRISTMAS DINNER

Red Wine—Poached Eggs with Seared Foie Gras and Potato Rösti

I brought this dish back from the Domaine de Châteauvieux in Geneva. The Swiss regard the potato rösti as some sort of national treasure. When you pair it with foie gras and white truffles, you'll see why.

SERVES 6 TO 8

POTATO RÖSTI
4 tbsp (60 mL) butter
4 tbsp (60 mL) grapeseed oil
2 lb (1 kg) potatoes, peeled and
    grated lengthwise

FOIE GRAS
1 tsp (5 mL) grapeseed oil
4 slices foie gras
½ cup (125 mL) red wine
¼ cup (50 mL) apple cider vinegar
1 cup (250 mL) dark chicken stock (see p. 216)
2 tbsp (30 mL) butter
Salt and pepper to taste

MUSHROOMS
1 cup (250 mL) black trumpet
    (or any quality wild) mushrooms
1 large shallot, finely chopped
1 clove garlic, finely chopped
2 tbsp (30 mL) butter
Salt and pepper to taste

POACHED EGGS
3 cups (750 mL) heavy red wine
¼ cup (50 mL) red wine vinegar
Pinch of salt
8 whole eggs

GARNISH
Pinch of minced chives
2 tsp (10 mL) slivered white truffle (optional)

Preheat the oven to 375°F (190°C).

Melt 2 tbsp (30 mL) of the butter and 2 tbsp (30 mL) of the grapeseed oil in a large cast-iron pan over medium heat. Add the potatoes and carefully blend with the fat. Using a palette knife, pack the potatoes evenly. Bake for 20 minutes. Carefully flip the potatoes over and, before returning to the oven, place the remaining butter and grapeseed oil along the edges of the pan. Cook 15 minutes longer until golden brown and cooked through. Remove from oven and carefully flip onto a cutting board.

For the foie gras, heat the grapeseed oil in a frying pan over high heat. Sear the foie gras on both sides until soft. Remove the foie gras and set aside. Deglaze the pan with the red wine and apple cider vinegar. Reduce by three-quarters and pour in a saucepan. Add the dark chicken stock and reduce by one-quarter. Swirl in the butter and season with salt and pepper to taste. Set aside.

In a hot pan over high heat, sauté the mushrooms, shallots, and garlic in the butter. Season to taste and spoon onto dry paper towel to drain.

Bring the red wine to a simmer with the vinegar and salt. Poach the eggs 2 at a time for 2 to 3 minutes. Remove with a slotted spoon and keep warm.

Using a 2-inch (5 cm) round cookie cutter, cut rounds from the rösti. In 4 small bowls, place the rösti rounds with foie gras on top, then the 2 poached eggs. Sprinkle the black trumpets around, drizzle with sauce, and garnish with chives. Finish with a few slivers of white truffle if desired.

Duck Fat–Fried Eggs with Périgord Truffles

Eggs and truffles make an ideal marriage.

SERVES 4

2 tbsp (30 mL) duck fat
2 eggs
1 black Périgord truffle
Sel de Guérande and freshly ground pepper to taste

In a nonstick pan, heat the duck fat. Fry the eggs sunny side up.

Carefully place the eggs in the centre of a plate and drizzle them lightly with duck fat. Use a truffle slicer to garnish them generously with black truffle. Season to taste.

Roasted Wagyu Marrow Bones
with a Warm Truffle Vinaigrette

This is a rich, superbly succulent, high-fat dish. But it's wintertime, and we all need a little extra padding.

SERVES 4

12 pieces Wagyu marrow bones
2 cups (500 mL) white wine
Juice of 1 lemon
2 shallots, chopped
3 tbsp (45 mL) water
6 tbsp (90 mL) very cold cubed butter
3 tbsp (45 mL) champagne vinegar
1 tsp (5 mL) black truffle
Salt and pepper to taste
16 baguette slices
Sprinkle of fleur de sel

Preheat the oven to 375°F (190°C).

Soak the marrow bones in lukewarm water for 24 hours, changing the water at least 4 times. Dry the bones with a cloth and stand them in a roasting tray. Bake for 15 to 20 minutes or until a skewer passes through the marrow with no resistance. Set aside.

For the warm truffle vinaigrette, mix the white wine, lemon juice, and shallots in a heavy saucepan and bring to a simmer. Reduce until nearly dry. Add the water and whisk in the very cold butter. Bring to a simmer while continuously whisking until creamy. Pass through a fine sieve, making sure to press all the flavour out of the shallots. Add the vinegar and the truffles; season to taste.

Place the baguette slices on a baking tray and brush with melted butter. Bake at 350°F (180°C) until crispy.

Place 3 hot Kobe bone marrows in the middle of 4 plates. Pour some of the warm truffle vinaigrette in each of the bone cavities. Arrange the toasted baguette slices on the plates, with the leftover vinaigrette and fleur de sel on the side.

Savoury Crêpes Stuffed with Apples, Onions, and Boudin Noir

I am obsessive about making my own charcuterie. Boudin noir is my favourite sausage—to eat and to make.

SERVES 4

CRÊPES

1 cup (250 mL) all-purpose flour

3 eggs

2 cups (500 mL) milk

2 tbsp (30 mL) sugar

1 tsp (5 mL) salt

2 tbsp (30 mL) melted butter

1 tbsp (15 mL) each chopped fresh thyme, chervil, and chives

STUFFING

2 tbsp (30 mL) chopped speck (or lightly smoked bacon)

2 tbsp (30 mL) duck fat

4 apples, peeled and diced

1 onion, julienned

4 whole boudin noir (blood sausage)

4 tsp (20 mL) butter

4 whole pickled crabapples (optional)

SAUCE

2 shallots, finely chopped

1 tsp (5 mL) finely chopped garlic

4 tsp (20 mL) butter

¼ cup (50 mL) port

⅔ cup (150 mL) veal jus (see p. 223)

12 snails

Salt and pepper to taste

Pinch of chives to garnish

Preheat the oven to 300°F (150°C).

To make the crêpes, whisk the flour and the eggs in a large mixing bowl. Gradually add the milk, stirring to combine. Whisk in the sugar, salt, butter, and chopped herbs until well combined. Set aside for at least 1 hour.

Melt a little butter in an 8-inch (20 cm) nonstick pan over medium heat. Ladle about ½ cup (125 mL) of the batter into the pan and tilt the pan with a circular motion so it coats the surface evenly. Cook the crêpe for 2 to 3 minutes, until the bottom is light brown. Loosen with a plastic spatula, flip the crêpe, and cook the other side. Make 4 crêpes and set aside for stuffing.

For the stuffing, sauté the speck in the duck fat until lightly browned. Mix in the apple and onion and cook until soft. Divide the stuffing equally among the 4 crêpes. Place 1 boudin noir in each and roll like a wrap. Lay on a baking sheet lined with parchment paper and bake for 15 minutes or until the boudin noir is hot. Slice each crêpe in half on the bias.

Meanwhile, in a saucepan over medium heat, sweat the shallots and garlic in 1½ tsp (7 mL) of the butter until translucent. Raise heat, deglaze with port, and reduce by half. Pour in the veal jus and reduce by one-quarter. Add the snails and bring to a simmer. Whisk in the remaining 2½ tsp (12 mL) butter and season with salt and pepper.

Arrange the crêpes on 4 plates, drizzle or glaze with sauce, and sprinkle with chives. If you choose, sauté the crabapples in the butter until heated through.

Tartine of Apple and Pear Chutney
with Truffled Pork Rillettes

François Rabelais called pork rillettes "brown pork jam." Good point. Why not spread it on a tartine?

SERVES 4

TRUFFLED PORK RILLETTE
1 cup (250 mL) water
14 oz (400 g) rendered pork fat
2 lb (1 kg) pork belly, diced
2 lb (1 kg) pork hind leg, diced
½ cup (125 mL) Alsatian Riesling
Sea salt and pepper to taste
1 oz (30 g) Périgord black truffles, chopped

APPLE AND PEAR CHUTNEY
2 cups (500 mL) apple cider vinegar
1½ cups (375 mL) old-fashioned brown sugar
8 McIntosh apples, peeled, cored, and chopped
7 Bosc pears, peeled, cored, and chopped
½ cup (125 mL) dried currants
1 cup (250 mL) coarsely chopped onion
⅓ cup (75 mL) peeled, finely chopped gingerroot
2 lemons, seeded and coarsely chopped with rind
1 tbsp (15 mL) chopped fresh mint
Sea salt to taste

TARTINE
4 slices sourdough bread
1 tbsp (15 mL) softened butter
4 small bunches red radish sprouts
12 Périgord black truffle slices

Preheat the oven to 220°F (100°C).

In a heavy-bottomed saucepan, bring the water to a simmer. Add the rendered fat, pork belly, and pork leg. Cover with a tight-fitting lid or foil. Place in a bain-marie and cook in the oven for 6 hours or until the meat is very tender.

Pour in the wine and return to the oven for another 45 minutes. Remove from the oven and mash the meat with a fork. Season with salt and pepper, then stir in the chopped truffles. Scrape the finished rillette into a jar. Let cool and refrigerate.

To make the apple and pear chutney, bring the vinegar and brown sugar to a simmer in a heavy saucepan. Stir in the apples, pears, currants, onion, gingerroot, lemon, mint, and sea salt to taste. Simmer, stirring occasionally, until thick. Pour into a jar and allow to cool.

Butter the bread slices. Spread with an even layer of apple and pear chutney. Arrange the red radish sprouts on top, followed by 2 quenelles (egg-shaped servings) of rillette. Garnish with slices of Périgord black truffles.

Duck Confit Panini with Grilled Oyster Mushrooms and Red Onion Balsamic Jam

Ciabatta to the Italians is what the baguette is to the French. At Petite Thuet all our panini are made with ciabatta prepared with a sourdough starter.

SERVES 2

RED ONION BALSAMIC JAM
1 tbsp (15 mL) grapeseed oil
3 red onions, finely sliced
4 tbsp (60 mL) balsamic (or other top-quality) vinegar
4 tsp (20 mL) organic clover honey
1½ tsp (7 mL) old-fashioned brown sugar

PANINI
2 ciabatta buns
3 tsp (15 mL) softened butter
4 slices Migneron de Charlevoix cheese
10 oz (300 g) shredded duck confit (see p. 121)
4 oz (120 g) grilled oyster mushrooms, seasoned
12 arugula leaves

Heat the grapeseed oil in a cast-iron pan over high heat. Add the red onions and cook until caramelized, stirring often. Transfer to a heavy-bottomed saucepan.

Add the balsamic vinegar and bring to a simmer. Stir in the clover honey and old-fashioned brown sugar and slowly simmer until the mixture reaches jam consistency.

Slice the ciabatta buns in half. Spread both sides with butter, followed by red onion balsamic jam. Lay a slice of cheese on the bottom of the buns, followed by the shredded duck confit, grilled oyster mushrooms, arugula, and another slice of Migneron de Charlevoix. Add the tops of the buns and grill in a panini press for 5 minutes.

NOTE: Migneron de Charlevoix is a highly popular cheese in Quebec from cheesemaker Maurice Dufour. If your cheesemaker doesn't carry it, request a different semi-soft, washed-rind, cow's milk cheese.

The croque monsieur is more familiar, but I prefer the croque madame—especially
my version, where Gruyère makes way for Pied-de-Vent, and the package is enhanced
with truffles.

SERVES 4

BÉCHAMEL
3 tbsp (45 mL) butter
4 tsp (20 mL) all-purpose flour
2 cups (500 mL) cold milk
Salt, pepper, and grated nutmeg to taste

CROQUE MADAME
8 pieces challah bread
16 thin slices Pied-de-Vent cheese
8 thin slices smoked ham
1 cup (250 mL) butter
4 eggs
Shaved truffle pieces and pinch of
    chives to garnish

Preheat the oven to 375°F (190°C).

For the béchamel, melt the butter in a saucepan over medium heat. Add the flour, stirring continuously with a wooden spoon until golden. Slowly whisk in the cold milk and bring to a gentle simmer. Reduce the heat to low and continue stirring for 4 to 5 minutes. Season with the salt, pepper, and nutmeg to taste and refrigerate until ready to use.

For the croque madame, spread béchamel on each piece of challah. Lay the slices of Pied-de-Vent cheese on top of the béchamel. Place the smoked ham slices on half of each sandwich and top with the remaining side.

Heat 2 nonstick pans and melt ½ cup (125 mL) of the butter in each. Place 2 sandwiches in each frying pan and brown both sides of the croque. Bake in the oven for 3 to 5 minutes or until the cheese melts. Meanwhile, in another large frying pan, fry the eggs sunny side up in a little butter. Place the croque mesdames on 4 plates. Top each with an egg and garnish with shaved truffles and chives.

NOTE   Reblochon cheese can be substituted for Pied-de-Vent if necessary, and Gruyère will work in a pinch.

Gratin of Tripe, Snails, and Foie Gras

This is Bee's favourite dish. There's nothing more to say.

SERVES 4

1 large onion, finely chopped

4 shallots, finely chopped

½ cup (125 mL) butter

28 oz (800 g) tripe, cleaned, blanched, and cut into 3-inch (8 cm) strips

1 sprig thyme

1 sprig oregano

2 cups (500 mL) Alsatian Riesling

2 cups (500 mL) chicken stock (see p. 215)

Sea salt, pepper, and ground four-spice mix to taste

2 carrots, peeled and sliced in thin rounds

2 tomatoes, peeled, seeded, and diced

12 snails, rinsed

2 tbsp (30 mL) chopped chives

1½ tsp (7 mL) finely chopped fresh tarragon

Bread crumbs for sprinkling

4 3-oz (90 g) slices foie gras

1½ tsp (7 mL) grapeseed oil

In an enamel pot, sauté the onions and shallots in ⅓ cup (75 mL) of the butter.

Add the tripe, thyme, and oregano. Cover with the white wine and chicken stock; season to taste with sea salt, pepper, and four-spice mix. Cook for approximately 2 hours over low heat, adding the carrots, tomatoes, and snails after 1½ hours. Add more stock to moisten if necessary. At the end of the cooking time, sprinkle in the chopped chives and tarragon. Season to taste.

Divide among 4 oven-safe dishes and top with bread crumbs and the remaining butter. Broil until golden brown.

Meanwhile, in a hot cast-iron pan, sear the foie gras slices in the grapeseed oil for 1½ minutes on each side, until medium-rare.

Delicately place the foie gras on top of the tripe gratin. Serve.

NOTE: Four-spice mix is usually a mixture of white pepper, nutmeg, ginger, and cinnamon or cloves, all in roughly equal proportions. If you don't want to buy a batch, simply use a pinch of each of its constituent parts.

Scott's Prison Chicken

One day I asked my cook Scott to make the staff lunch and he came up with Scott's Prison Chicken. My wife tried it and went on to polish off the entire staff meal. That's when I knew he had a winning recipe and asked him to contribute it to my book.

SERVES 8

2 whole free-range chickens, quartered (or any arrangement of chicken you might have: legs or thighs, boneless breasts)
Salt and pepper to taste
A cup or so (250 mL) soy sauce, dark or light
A spoonful or so of raw honey (you can substitute pancake syrup if necessary or even brown sugar)

A squirt of hoisin sauce if you have it, or perhaps ketchup or mustard (works well either way)
A shot or two of any hot sauce and/or some crushed chili flakes to your own liking
A squeeze of lemon (or a splash of O.J.)
A clove of fresh garlic, crushed (or a little fresh ginger, shredded), although I usually use the powdered kind

Preheat the oven to 350–375°F (177–191°C).

I like to roll the chicken in a little sesame oil before baking it to give it a nice crispy skin, but any oil will do (likewise none at all, if you prefer).

Season chicken with salt and pepper and place in the preheated oven (a BBQ works as well).

Whisk together the rest of the ingredients and modify to taste. If your soy was high in sodium, you may want to sweeten it a li'l more. If it seems too sweet, try a little more hot sauce or acid to balance out the flavour.

Allow chicken to cook approximately 15 minutes (or almost through), then drizzle or glaze with mixture. Cook for 5 minutes, then flip and repeat on the other side. Same method on a BBQ over medium heat, turning and glazing chicken until it has a nicely finished skin and is cooked thoroughly.

Then enjoy.

Coq au Riesling is found in every bistro in Alsace. It's usually served with homemade pasta or spätzle. Here I make it with capon.

SERVES 4

1 capon, cut into 8 serving pieces
3 cups (750 mL) Alsatian Riesling
1 small white onion, chopped
1 carrot, chopped
1 sprig of rosemary
1 sprig of thyme
1 bay leaf
2 tbsp (30 mL) grapeseed oil
2 cloves of garlic
½ cup cognac
1 cup (250 mL) chicken stock (see p. 215)
Salt and pepper to taste
12 oz (350 g) speck (or lightly smoked bacon), chopped
8 seasonal mushrooms, sliced
1 cup (250 mL) whipping cream
Sprinkle of chives to garnish

FETTUCCINE
3½ oz (100 g) fettuccine
Salt and pepper to taste
2 tbsp (30 mL) whipping cream
1 tbsp (15 mL) soft butter

A day in advance, clean and cut the capon in 8 pieces or more. Put it in a large bowl and pour in the Riesling. Stir in the onions, carrots, rosemary, thyme, and bay leaf. Cover and refrigerate overnight. The next day, drain the capon and vegetables, reserving the wine.

In a large skillet, brown the capon pieces in the grapeseed oil. Remove the capon. Add the garlic and reserved vegetables to the pot and heat through for a couple of minutes. Transfer the capon and vegetables to a large saucepan on high heat. Pour in the cognac and flambé. When the flame dies, add the reserved wine, chicken stock, and salt and pepper to taste. Lower heat to medium and bring to a boil. Cover and simmer for 1½ to 2 hours.

In a small skillet, sauté the speck and mushrooms until brown, about 10 minutes. Add to the pot (once the chicken is cooked). Pour in the whipping cream and cook, stirring, for 2 or 3 minutes. Taste and correct the seasoning, and garnish with chives.

In a large pot of boiling salted water, cook the fettuccine until al dente. Drain well and place in a mixing bowl. Season with salt and pepper. Stir in the whipping cream and butter. Toss the pasta and place in a serving dish.

Serve the capon from its pot at the table—it's the best way to enjoy it.

Civet of Wild Venison with Fresh Spätzle

I dedicate this recipe to my uncle Pierro—an avid hunter, my first chef, and a man immensely devoted to the culinary craft. At the tender age of 82, he still helps my cousin butcher wild boar, deer, and hare, but also finds the time to peel asparagus at the peak of the spring season.

SERVES 4

SPÄTZLE
2 cups (500 mL) flour
2 cups (500 mL) milk
6 eggs
3 tbsp (45 mL) butter
Salt, pepper, and nutmeg to taste

VENISON CIVET
7 lb (3 kg) venison (neck and shoulder meat), cubed
3 cups (750 mL) red wine
2 carrots, roughly chopped
1 onion, quartered
4 garlic cloves, peeled and crushed
8 juniper berries, crushed

3 bay leaves
2 sprigs thyme
1½ tsp (7 mL) whole black peppercorns
4 tbsp (60 mL) grapeseed oil
3 tbsp (45 mL) flour
Salt and pepper to taste
4 tbsp (60 mL) butter
16 pearl onions
Pinch of sugar
½ cup (125 mL) speck (or lightly smoked bacon), chopped
1 tbsp (15 mL) grapeseed oil
1 cup (250 mL) sliced mushrooms
2 tbsp (30 mL) gin

Preheat the oven to 375°F (190°C).

SPÄTZLE

Combine the flour, milk, and eggs in a stand mixer with the paddle attachment. Mix until the dough is homogenized and a little runny. Let the dough rest for an hour. Bring 5 quarts (5 L) of salted water to a boil. With a spatula, force the dough through a large-holed colander into the boiling water. Cook until the spätzle float to the surface, 4 to 5 minutes. Remove with a slotted spoon and immediately transfer to an ice bath to stop the cooking.

In a large, hot sauté pan, melt the butter and add the spätzle, cooking until golden brown. Season with salt, pepper, and nutmeg. Set aside.

VENISON CIVET

Stir together the venison, red wine, carrots, onion, garlic, juniper berries, bay leaves, thyme, and peppercorns in a large mixing bowl. Marinate in the fridge for 48 hours. Two hours before searing the meat, drain through a colander, reserving the liquid and venison/vegetable mixture separately.

In a large cast-iron pan, sear the venison in grapeseed oil until golden brown. Transfer to a large enamel pot. Next, sear all the vegetables from the marinade and transfer to the enamel pot. Sprinkle with the flour. Roast uncovered in the oven for 10 minutes until the flour starts to change colour. Pour the reserved marinade liquid over the meat, making sure it's completely covered. Season with salt and pepper to taste. On the stovetop, bring everything to a simmer, cover, and return to the oven for 2 hours or until the meal is tender. Remove meat from the pot and set aside, covered. Pass braising liquid through a chinois into a saucepan. Discard the vegetables, bay leaves, and thyme.

Reduce liquid by three-quarters over medium heat. Swirl in 2 tbsp (30 mL) of the butter; season to taste. Add the venison and set aside.

To make the sauce, melt the remaining butter in a sauté pan over high heat. Sauté the pearl onions with a pinch of sugar until caramelized. Deglaze with a little water and repeat until the pearl onions soften.

In a separate pan, sauté the speck in grapeseed oil until crispy. Set aside. In the same pan, sauté the mushrooms until soft. Mix the onions, speck, and mushrooms.

Bring the meat back to a simmer and stir in the gin. Pour the meat and sauce into a deep serving platter. Top with the pearl onions, speck, and mushrooms. Serve with the spätzle on a separate platter.

NOTE: Can also be served with poached pears (1 per serving).

Beef Carpaccio with Vacherin Mont-d'Or, Tête de Moine, and Black Truffles

Watches aside, Switzerland's finest exports must be horse carpaccio and Vacherin Mont d'Or. My brother Serge lives in Zurich, and every Christmas when he visits he brings me one in its fragrant spruce box. These four flavours go together beautifully, whether you use beef or horse carpaccio.

SERVES 4

8 oz (225 g) beef fillet
Juice of 2 lemons
2 tbsp (30 mL) olive oil
2 mangosteens
2 tbsp (30 mL) Vacherin Mont-d'Or

4 Tête de Moine rosettes, prepared
    with a Girolle
1 cup (250 mL) torn frisée
2½ oz (75 g) black truffles, sliced
Fleur de sel and pepper to taste

Place the beef fillet in the freezer until it becomes firm, but don't freeze it completely. Thinly slice using a meat slicer and arrange the slices in an overlapping circle on 4 plates.

In a mixing bowl whisk together the lemon juice, olive oil, and a pinch of fleur de sel. Set aside.

Using a sharp knife, cut around the circumference of each mangosteen. Take it with both hands and pry open the fruit. Remove the white segments.

Place ½ tbsp (12 mL) of the Vacherin Mont-d'Or in the centre of each carpaccio serving. Next to this place the Tête de Moine rosettes and torn frisée. Drizzle the carpaccio with the olive oil/lemon juice mixture. Garnish with mangosteen wedges and black truffle slices. Immediately before serving, sprinkle with fleur de sel and pepper.

NOTE: The mangosteen is a purple-skinned, juicy fruit from Southeast Asia that's available at most Asian markets around Christmastime—like Vacherin Mont-d'Or, a rich, runny, cow's-milk cheese made in France or Switzerland. Tête de Moine is a Swiss cheese that literally translates as "monk's head" (it was a tithe). A Girolle is a utensil used to scrape the Tête de Moine cheese into rosettes.

Hand-Rolled Potato Gnocchi with Braised Veal Cheeks, Black Truffles, and Poached Quail Eggs

My preferred comfort food for a cold winter's night.

SERVES 4

GNOCCHI
3 large potatoes
Coarse sea salt to taste
2½ tbsp (37 mL) olive oil
Fine sea salt to taste
1–1¼ cups (250–300 mL) all-purpose flour
1 egg

BRAISED VEAL CHEEKS
4 veal cheeks, trimmed of excess fat
Salt and pepper to taste
1 tbsp (15 mL) canola oil
1 shallot, chopped
½ onion, chopped
½ leek, chopped (white part only)
½ carrot, chopped
1 bay leaf (fresh if possible)
1 sprig thyme
½ cup (125 mL) Alsatian Riesling
1½ cups (375 mL) veal jus (see p. 223)
½ cup (125 mL) bread crumbs
1 tbsp (15 mL) chopped chives
1½ tsp (7 mL) chopped chervil
1 tbsp (15 mL) Dijon mustard
1 tbsp (15 mL) butter
1½ oz (45 g) black truffles, sliced

POACHED QUAIL EGGS
1 tbsp (15 mL) white wine vinegar
Pinch of salt
4 quail eggs

GNOCCHI

Place the potatoes on top of a small baking sheet covered with coarse sea salt. Bake at 375°F (190°C) for 1 hour or until soft. Set aside and let cool slightly.

Peel the baked potatoes and pass through a potato ricer onto a flour-dusted work surface. Drizzle the olive oil over the potatoes. Add a small pinch of fine sea salt.

Next, mix in the flour in small amounts until blended. Make a well in the centre of the mixture and crack the egg into it. Mix the egg with your fingertips to gather the potato and flour mixture into the egg a little at a time. If the dough is very sticky, add more flour.

When the dough is smooth and slightly tacky, knead in another pinch of fine sea salt. Cut the dough into 6 equal pieces and roll into balls. Clean your work surface and lightly dust with flour. Roll each portion of dough to form a long sausage ¼ inch (5 mm) thick. Cut each roll into ½-inch (1 cm) pieces. Place the gnocchi on a tray lined with parchment paper and refrigerate.

BRAISED VEAL CHEEKS

Season the veal cheeks well with salt and pepper. Heat the canola oil in a cast-iron pan over high heat. Sear the veal cheeks for 2 minutes on each side. Remove and place in an enamel pot.

Reduce the heat and sauté the shallots, onions, leeks, carrots, bay leaf, and thyme sprig until golden brown. Deglaze with the white wine and bring to a simmer. Add the veal jus and return to a simmer. Pour the braising liquid over the veal cheeks in the enamel pot, cover, and bake at 350°F (180°C) for 1½ hours or until you can put a skewer through the meat with no resistance.

Remove the cheeks and strain the braising liquid through cheesecloth. Return the liquid to a saucepan on medium heat and reduce to 1 cup (250 mL).

In a mixing bowl, combine the bread crumbs, ½ tbsp (7 mL) of the chives, and the chervil. Brush the veal cheeks with mustard and roll in the bread crumb mixture. Bake at 350°F (180°C) until crispy. Set aside.

TO FINISH

Cook the gnocchi in batches in a well-salted pot of boiling water. When the gnocchi floats to the surface, it is cooked. Remove with a slotted spoon and place in a lightly oiled, warm bowl.

Pour the sauce in 2 large frying pans over medium heat and bring to a light simmer. Whisk ½ tbsp (7 mL) butter in each pan. Toss half the gnocchi in the sauce in each pan. Season to taste.

Divide the gnocchi among 4 pasta bowls. Place the veal cheeks on top in the centre and garnish with the remaining chives and the truffle slices.

To make the poached eggs, add the white vinegar and salt to a small pot of water and bring to a light simmer. Break each quail egg into a small cup without breaking the yolks. Gently pour each egg into the simmering water and poach for 45 to 60 seconds. Carefully remove with a slotted spoon and immediately place the poached eggs on top of the plated veal cheeks.

Choucroute à l'Alsacienne

The first memory I have of choucroute is my grandmother stewing her soured cabbage in the cellar (the room smells of it to this day). Choucroute isn't just an Alsatian dish—it's *the* dish of every Alsatian.

SERVES 4

SAUERKRAUT
4 garlic cloves
3 cloves
1 bay leaf
1 sprig of thyme
8 juniper berries
20 black peppercorns
2 lb (1 kg) sauerkraut
1 white onion, sliced
7 oz (200 g) duck or goose fat
2 cups (500 mL) Riesling

2 cups (500 mL) chicken stock (see p. 215)
1 smoked pork hock
10 oz (300 g) speck (or lightly smoked bacon), sliced
7 oz (200 g) kessler (smoked pork shoulder)
Sel de Guérande to taste
4 small russet potatoes
7 oz (200 g) Montbéliard sausage
10 oz (300 g) jaggerwurst (hunter's sausage)
10 oz (300 g) boudin blanc (white sausage)
10 oz (300 g) boudin noir (blood sausage)

Preheat the oven to 350°F (180°C).

Place the garlic cloves, cloves, bay leaf, thyme sprig, juniper berries, and peppercorns in the centre of a small piece of cheesecloth; tie the tops together with string to form a pouch. Wash the sauerkraut multiple times and squeeze to press out all the liquid.

In a deep enamel pot, sauté the onion in 5 oz (150 g) of the duck fat until translucent. Pour in the Riesling and chicken stock, bringing to a simmer. Add the pork hock, speck, kessler, sauerkraut, and spice pouch. Season to taste with sel de Guérande. Cover and cook in the oven for 30 minutes. Add the potatoes and return to the oven for another hour.

Bring a large pot of water to a boil. Add the Montbéliard, jaggerwurst, and boudin blanc and cook for 10 minutes. Set aside.

In an oven-safe skillet, heat the remaining duck fat and sear the boudin noir on all sides for 3 minutes. Place the skillet in the oven for 7 minutes.

To serve, remove all the meats from the pot, discarding the spice pouch. Remove the bone from the pork hock and slice the meat in 4 portions. Slice the kessler and the speck in 4 portions. Loosely drain the sauerkraut and place it in the centre of a large platter, arranging the meat and sausages on top. Place the potatoes along the edges of the platter. Serve at the table.

Pieds de Porc Farcis with Creamed Potato and Red Wine Reduction

"Dans le cochon, tout est bon." This extravagant Alsatian proverb translates as "In the pig, everything is good." This recipe is a testament to that.

SERVES 4

PIEDS DE PORC
3 tbsp (45 mL) butter
1 carrot, peeled and diced
1 onion, diced
2 garlic cloves, peeled and crushed
4 tsp (20 mL) brown sugar
3 tbsp (45 mL) aged red wine vinegar
¼ cup (50 mL) port
2 hind pig trotters, deboned
1⅔ cups (400 mL) chicken stock (see p. 215)
2 cups (500 mL) veal jus (see p. 223)
1 sprig thyme
1¼ cups (300 mL) water
2½ oz (75 g) black truffles, sliced
Salt and pepper to taste

FARCE (STUFFING)
7 oz (200 g) raw chicken breast, diced
2 egg whites
¾ cup (175 mL) whipping cream
2½ oz (75 g) black trumpets, trimmed, washed, and patted dry
1 tsp (5 mL) grapeseed oil
2½ oz (75 g) fresh foie gras, diced
1½ tsp (7 mL) chopped chives
Salt and pepper to taste

CREAMED POTATOES
2 lb (1 kg) baking potatoes, skin left on
1 cup (250 mL) whipping cream
1 cup (250 mL) butter
Salt, pepper, and nutmeg to taste

Preheat the oven to 350°F (180°C).

PIEDS DE PORC
In a large, heavy enamel pot, melt 2 tbsp (30 mL) of the butter over medium heat. Brown the carrots, onions, and garlic. Add the brown sugar and caramelize. Deglaze with the red wine vinegar and reduce to dry. Add the port and the trotters. Reduce the heat and turn the trotters until they are well coated with the syrup.

Pour in the chicken and veal stock. Add the sprig of thyme and bring to a simmer. Cover and roast in the oven for 3 hours, turning the trotters every 30 minutes.

Remove from the oven. Lift the trotters onto a buttered piece of foil. With a spoon, carefully scrape out excess fat from inside the trotters. Leave to cool at room temperature.

Add the water to the braising liquid. Pass the liquid through cheesecloth, making sure to squeeze as much juice and flavour as possible from the vegetables. Pour into a saucepan and set aside.

FARCE
In a food processor, purée the chicken breast with the egg whites and 2 pinches of salt. Transfer the bowl of mixture to the refrigerator for an hour.

Return the bowl to the food processor. Blend in the chilled cream, adding a little at a time. Force the meat through a fine sieve and refrigerate again.

In a frying pan, sauté the black trumpets in the grapeseed oil. Season to taste and remove from the pan onto paper towel to cool. Once cool, add the trumpets, foie gras, and chives to the mousse, mixing with a wooden spoon.

Stuff the trotters by spooning the farce into the hoof cavity. Reshape the trotters and wrap them tightly in buttered foil twice, twisting the ends to ensure they're tightly wrapped. Place in the fridge for an hour.

Bring a large pot of water to a simmer. Add the foiled trotters and bake in a 350°F (180°C) oven for 30 to 40 minutes, or until the farce is cooked. Remove and place the trotters on a carving board.

CREAMED POTATOES

Put the potatoes in a large pot and cover with cold, salted water. Bring to a boil and simmer over high heat until the potatoes are tender, 35 to 40 minutes. Drain and peel the potatoes. Rice the potatoes in a potato ricer.

Bring the cream and butter to a simmer in a small pot. Slowly stir into the potatoes with a wooden spoon. Season with salt, pepper, and nutmeg to taste. Set aside.

TO FINISH

Bring the braising liquid to a simmer and skim. Reduce to 1 cup (250 mL). Add the truffles and correct the seasoning. Whisk in the remaining tablespoon of butter.

Divide the creamed potatoes among 4 plates. Unwrap the trotters and halve vertically. Place on top of the potatoes. Glaze the trotters with the truffle-spiked sauce and serve.

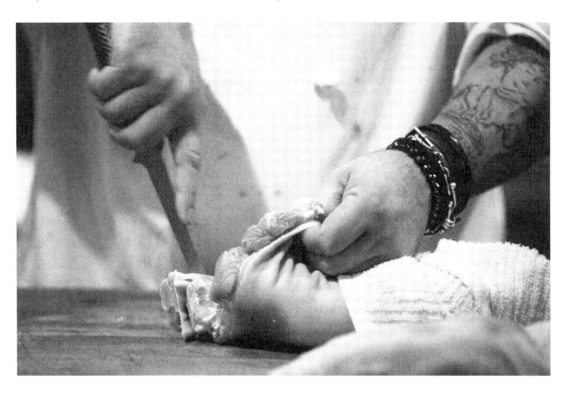

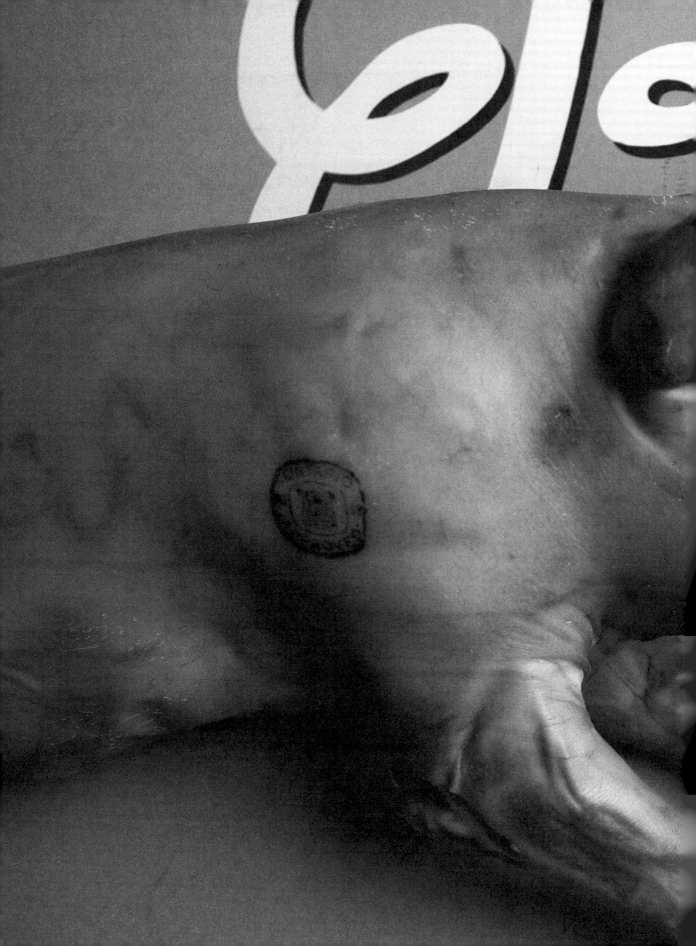

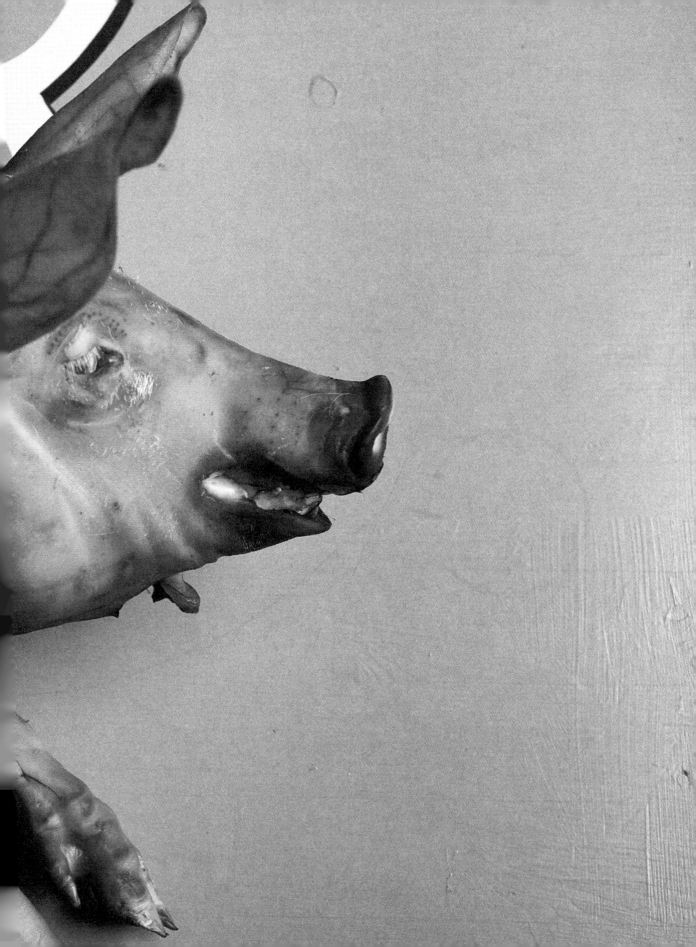

This is my special version of the classic duck à l'orange. For me, this recipe is the link to Christmas and the wonderful memory of my grandmother's famed foie gras terrine.

SERVES 4

BEIGNETS

1 cup (250 mL) all-purpose flour, sifted

Pinch of salt

²/₃ cup (150 mL) Chambly Noire (or other dark ale)

1 tbsp (15 mL) olive oil

1½ tsp (7 mL) dry yeast

1 small egg white, stiffly beaten

4 small crabapples, peeled, stems on

¼ cup (50 mL) Calvados

2 tbsp (30 mL) sugar

Canola oil, for deep-frying

SALSIFY PURÉE

3 salsify stalks, peeled and chopped in 1-inch (2.5 cm) pieces

3 cups (750 mL) milk

4 tbsp (60 mL) butter

¼ tsp (1 mL) sugar

½ cup (125 mL) whipping cream

½ vanilla bean, scraped

Salt and pepper to taste

MUSHROOMS

4 oz (120 g) slab bacon, cut in small cubes

1 tbsp (15 mL) finely chopped shallots

1 tsp (10 mL) finely chopped garlic

1 cup (250 mL) sliced canary (or any other seasonal wild) mushrooms

Salt and pepper to taste

GINGER AND BLOOD ORANGE REDUCTION

⅓ cup (75 mL) sugar

3 tbsp (45 mL) butter

Juice of 2 blood oranges

Juice of 1 lemon

1 tbsp (10 mL) rice wine vinegar

1 cup (250 mL) duck jus (see p. 219)

1 tsp (10 mL) chopped gingerroot

2 tbsp (30 mL) butter

Salt and pepper to taste

DUCK MAGRET

2 tbsp (30 mL) buckwheat (or other quality liquid) honey

2 tbsp (30 mL) rice wine vinegar

4 Magret of duck

1 tbsp (15 mL) grapeseed oil

8 blood orange segments, peeled, membrane removed

Preheat the oven to 250°F (120°C).

BEIGNETS

Marinate the crabapples with the Calvados and sugar overnight.

To make the batter, mix the sifted flour and salt in a warm bowl. Make a well in the centre of the flour and pour in the lukewarm ale, olive oil, and yeast. Mix well. Cover the bowl and allow the mixture to rest 5 to 6 hours. Fold in the stiffly beaten egg white.

Coat the marinated apples carefully in the batter, making sure the stems stay attached and dry. Fry the beignets in the hot canola oil in a medium-sized saucepan for 3 minutes until golden brown. Remove and drain on paper towel.

SALSIFY PURÉE

In a saucepan over medium heat, poach the salsify in the milk for 15 to 20 minutes or until tender. Strain and pat dry.

Heat 2 tbsp (30 mL) of the butter in a sauté pan over medium heat. Sauté the salsify with the sugar until golden brown.

Meanwhile, bring the cream and vanilla to a simmer and let infuse for 15 minutes. Remove the vanilla bean and pour the cream into a blender. Add the sautéed salsify and remaining 2 tbsp (30 mL) butter. Purée until smooth; season with salt and pepper.

MUSHROOMS

In a sauté pan, sauté the bacon until crispy. Remove the bacon and add the shallots and garlic. Sauté until translucent. Add the mushrooms and sauté 4 to 5 minutes until tender. Season with salt and pepper to taste. Set aside.

GINGER AND BLOOD ORANGE REDUCTION

In a thick-bottomed saucepan, cook the sugar and butter over medium heat for approximately 3 minutes, until the sugar and butter become brown. Deglaze with the blood orange and lemon juice and rice wine vinegar. Reduce to syrup consistency.

Add the duck jus and gingerroot and reduce by one-quarter. Whisk in the butter and season to taste. Pass through a fine sieve and set aside.

DUCK MAGRET

Combine the buckwheat honey and rice wine vinegar on very low heat. Set aside.

In a hot skillet, sear the duck breasts skin side down in the grapeseed oil for 5 to 6 minutes. Flip the breasts and glaze the skin with the buckwheat honey/rice wine vinegar mixture. Bake in the preheated oven for 2 to 3 minutes. Remove from the pan and let rest on a cutting board.

TO FINISH

Spoon the salsify purée in the centre of 4 serving plates. Arrange the mushrooms around the purée. With a carving knife, thinly slice the duck magret on a bias and place the reconstructed duck magret on top of the salsify purée. Glaze the duck with blood orange and ginger sauce. Garnish with 2 blood orange segments per plate and place a crabapple beignet on top of the duck.

NOTE: Magret of duck refers to the breast meat of a duck that has been force-fed with corn for foie gras. Aux Champs d'Élisé Marieville, in Quebec, is a top Canadian supplier.

Deer Côtelette with Braised
Endives, Almond Coulis, Medjool
Dates, and Chocolate-Infused
Tangerine Reduction

The deer that I cook is the deer that I hunt. When I hunt, I enjoy the solitude of the forest—it's a rare opportunity to get some much-needed peace and quiet. This is one of my favourite recipes for a fresh catch.

SERVES 4

ROASTED ALMOND COULIS
¼ cup (50 mL) toasted slivered almonds
¼ cup (50 mL) whipping cream
½ cup (125 mL) milk
1½ tsp (7 mL) butter

BRAISED ENDIVES
2 endives
½ lemon, sliced
½ orange, sliced
Pinch of saffron
1½ tbsp (22 mL) butter
Juice of ½ lemon
Juice of ½ orange
1 tbsp (15 mL) chicken stock (see p. 215)
Salt, pepper, and sugar to taste

CHANTERELLES
1 cup (250 mL) whole chanterelles
   (or other seasonal wild mushrooms)
1 tbsp (15 mL) butter
2 shallots, finely diced
2 tsp (10 mL) chopped chervil

TANGERINE CHOCOLATE REDUCTION
½ cup (125 mL) freshly squeezed tangerine juice
1 cup (250 mL) veal jus (see p. 223)
2 juniper berries, crushed
4 Medjool dates, halved and pitted
1½ tsp (7 mL) butter
2 tsp (10 mL) finely grated 70% chocolate

VENISON
4 oz (120 g) venison chops
1 tbsp (15 mL) grapeseed oil
1 tbsp (15 mL) butter

ROASTED ALMOND COULIS
Combine the almonds, cream, milk, and butter in a saucepan. Bring to a slow simmer for 5 minutes, adding more milk if it becomes too thick. Once the almonds become soft, pour the hot mixture into a blender. Blend for 2 minutes or until smooth. Set aside.

BRAISED ENDIVES
Place the endives in a pressure cooker with the lemon and orange slices (otherwise cook conventionally at a boil for twice the time). Cover with water and a pinch of salt. Cook for 8 minutes. Remove the endives and halve lengthwise. Cut off the root ends and discard. Slice lengthwise in 1–inch-thick (2.5 cm) slices.

Place the saffron and ½ tbsp (7 mL) of the butter in a sauté pan over medium heat. After 30 seconds, add the lemon and orange juice, reducing by one-quarter. Stir in the chicken stock.

Add the endive slices. Whisk in 1 tbsp (15 mL) butter. Season with salt, pepper, and sugar to taste. Set aside.

CHANTERELLES
Sauté the chanterelles in butter until soft. Stir in the shallots; cook for 3 minutes and season to taste. Sprinkle with chervil and set aside.

TANGERINE CHOCOLATE REDUCTION
In a heavy-bottomed saucepan over medium heat, reduce tangerine juice by three-quarters, reserving 1 tbsp (15 mL). Stir in the veal stock and crushed juniper berries and reduce by half. Add the Medjool dates. Whisk in the butter. Add the finely grated chocolate and season with salt and pepper to taste. Set aside.

VENISON
Season the venison well with salt and pepper. In a hot sauté pan sear the venison chops in the grapeseed oil on both sides for about 3 minutes per side, basting occasionally. When you flip the chops, add the butter to the pan. Remove the venison from the pan and allow the meat to rest.

TO FINISH
Spoon a dollop of the roasted almond purée onto 4 round plates, using the back of the spoon to spread it in a semicircle near the outer edges. Place the braised endives in the centre and top with the venison chops. Arrange the chanterelles attractively around the plates.

Immediately before serving, add the reserved tablespoon of tangerine juice to the sauce. Spoon the sauce over the venison and place the halved Medjool dates on top of the chops.

Cassoulet à ma Façon

My take on cassoulet is essentially a combination of the three distinct traditions of Castelnaudary, Carcassonne, and Toulouse. The three have different meat content but use the same lingot beans, which render their cooking liquid thick and creamy, obviating the need for breadcrumbs to help the cassoulet form a surface crust. Tradition dictates that this crust should be cracked as it forms every twenty to thirty minutes—a total of seven times.

SERVES 6 TO 8

2 lb (1 kg) lingot (or coco or haricot) beans
1 lb (500 g) mildly smoked slab bacon, cut into thick 2-inch (4 cm) strips
2 quarts (2 L) white chicken stock
1 lb (500 g) pork shoulder or belly, cut into 1½- to 2-inch (3 to 4 cm) cubes
1 lb (500 g) lamb shoulder, cut into 1½- to 2-inch (3 to 4 cm) cubes

Salt, pepper
1 lb (500 g) Toulouse sausage (or other top-quality mildly seasoned pork sausage)
3 tbsp (45 mL) basic olive oil (or duck or goose fat)
4 garlic cloves, chopped
3 Roma tomatoes, concassé
2 legs duck confit

Preheat the oven to 325°F (160°C).

Soak the beans overnight in cold water. Drain, transfer to a large pot, and cover generously with fresh cold water. Bring to a boil for 5 minutes and then drain again. Return the beans to the pot with the bacon and add chicken stock to cover (you may have some left over). Bring to a boil and then lower heat and simmer gently, partly covered, until the beans begin to soften but are not losing their skins—about 1 hour. Drain the beans, but this time reserve the cooking liquid.

Generously season the pork and lamb. Heat a large skillet on medium-high, add the oil, and then sear the lamb, pork, and sausage until browned on all sides. Remove to a dish to drain and cool. Reserve the cooking fat.

To begin assembling the cassoulet, fold together the beans, garlic, and tomatoes in a large bowl. Season with salt and pepper. Transfer a third of the beans to the base of a cassoulet (or other heavy-bottomed casserole, preferably clay). Cut the sausages into 2-inch pieces. Arrange half the sausage, pork, and lamb on top of the first layer of beans. Follow with half the remaining beans, a second layer of meat, and finally the last beans. Carefully add the reserved bean-simmering liquid and lastly the cooking fat. Season, and transfer to the oven until the crust has formed and—after being cracked seven times—has turned golden-brown (about 2 to 2½ hours). Meanwhile, about 20 minutes before the cooking is complete, sear the duck legs skin-side down in a skillet on medium heat. Once the skin is crisp and brown, remove the legs to the cutting board, cut the meat from the bones in large chunks, and then arrange the pieces skin-side up on top of the cassoulet. When the cassoulet is ready and the duck thoroughly crisp and heated through, allow it to rest for 10 minutes before ladling it out at the table, preferably accompanied with crusty sourdough bread.

King Crab, Avocado, and Foie Gras Chantilly Roll with Sea Urchin Vinaigrette

The dangers of catching this majestic sea creature are well documented—these fishermen are true heroes of the hunt. Enjoy the privilege of feasting on king crab, and savour the sweetness of the sea.

SERVES 4

KING CRAB, AVOCADO, AND FOIE GRAS CHANTILLY ROLLS

12 oz (350 g) short-grain sushi rice
1¾ cups (425 mL) cold water
½ cup (125 mL) Japanese rice vinegar
1 tbsp plus 1 tsp (15 mL plus 5 mL) sea salt
1 tbsp (15 mL) mirin (sweet cooking wine)
1/3 cup (75 mL) granulated sugar
¾ cup (175 mL) milk
2½ oz (75 g) foie gras, cut in small cubes
Pinch of sugar
Salt and white pepper to taste
1 tsp (5 mL) ice wine
2 nori sheets
1 king crab leg, shelled, lightly poached
1 avocado, peeled and thinly sliced
Baby lettuce or sprouts to garnish (optional)

SEA URCHIN VINAIGRETTE

1 cup (250 mL) rice wine vinegar
1 cup (250 mL) sherry vinegar
½ cup (125 mL) grapeseed oil
1/3 cup (75 mL) walnut oil
2½ oz (75 g) sea urchin
1½ tsp (7 mL) Dijon mustard
4 tbsp (60 mL) lukewarm water

Wash the rice, rubbing and rinsing until the water is no longer cloudy. Cook the rice with the cold water in a rice cooker according to the manufacturer's instructions.

Meanwhile, make the sushi vinegar by gently heating the vinegar with the sea salt, mirin, and caster sugar until the salt and sugar are completely dissolved. Do not boil. Remove from heat and let cool.

Transfer the rice to a wooden mixing bowl and sprinkle with half the sushi vinegar. With a plastic rice paddle or spatula, incorporate the vinegar in a slicing motion into the rice. Make sure you don't overwork the rice as it will become too sticky. Once the rice has cooled, add the remaining vinegar mixture and repeat the slicing motion into the rice. Cover with a clean, wet cloth and use at room temperature within an hour.

To make the foie gras Chantilly, pour the milk into a heavy-bottomed saucepan. Add the foie gras and turn on low heat. Allow the foie gras to poach for 5 minutes or until very soft. Season with a pinch of sugar, salt, and white pepper. Stir in the ice wine and transfer to a blender. Blend until smooth, then cool in the fridge.

To assemble the nori rolls, place a small bowl of lukewarm water beside your workstation to dip your fingers into while working with the rice.

Lay the nori sheets on top of bamboo rolling mats. With wet fingers, spread the rice evenly, leaving a ½-inch (1 cm) border on the farthest side of the nori sheet. Put the cold foie gras Chantilly in a piping bag and pipe a line horizontally across the centre of the rice. Place a piece of king crab alongside the foie gras. Lift the end of the nori nearest you, with the help of the bamboo mat, and carefully roll it over the filling, pressing down as you go. You now have a nori roll.

Place plastic wrap on top of a bamboo mat and overlap the thin slices of avocado the same length as the nori sheet. Place the nori roll on top of the avocado, and while holding the bamboo mat and the plastic wrap, roll away from you. Press down on the rolling mat at both ends to secure the avocado to the nori roll.

For the sea urchin vinaigrette, mix the rice wine vinegar, sherry vinegar, grapeseed oil, walnut oil, sea urchin, and Dijon in a blender. Season to taste. Pour in a Mason jar, add the water, cover, and shake.

Slice each king crab roll, starting from the centre, into 6 pieces. Place 3 pieces in the centre of 4 plates and pour some vinaigrette around the rolls. Garnish with baby lettuce or sprouts, if desired.

Pot de Crème

Don't be intimidated by crème brûlée, or pot de crème in this case. Long revered, this dish was first served up in the late 1600s and has been re-created in French kitchens ever since. It's actually easy to make. There's always something special about breaking through the hard, caramelized sugar crust to get to the creamy custard that lies beneath.

SERVES 4

1½ cups (375 mL) whipping cream
3 tbsp (45 mL) milk
4 tbsp (60 mL) Rooibos de Provence (lavender-infused African Red Bush tea)
½ cup (125 mL) sugar
5 egg yolks
½ cup (125 mL) light brown sugar

Preheat the oven to 300°F (150°C).

Combine the cream and milk in a saucepan and bring to a simmer. Add the tea leaves and remove from heat. Let steep for 30 minutes. Strain through a fine sieve.

In a medium bowl, whisk the white sugar and egg yolks until pale yellow. While continuously whisking, gradually add the cream to the egg mixture.

Pour the custard into 4 ramekins placed in a baking pan, filling them three-quarters full. Pour enough boiling water to come halfway up the sides of the pan. Bake for 30 minutes or until the custard sets. Set aside and let cool completely in the fridge.

Preheat the broiler. Sprinkle brown sugar evenly on top of the cool custards and place under the broiler until caramelized. Let cool for 2 minutes and serve.

My grandmother used to make this fruit bread every year three to four weeks before Christmas—there'd be no Christmas in Alsace without it.

2 cups (500 mL) dried pears
¾ cup (175 mL) dried apples
¾ cup (175 mL) dried prunes
1 cup (250 mL) raisins
¾ cup (175 mL) currants
⅓ cup (75 mL) mixed citrus peel
½ cup (125 mL) chopped walnuts
⅓ cup (75 mL) chopped almonds
1 tsp (5 mL) cinnamon
1 tsp (5 mL) ground star anise
1¼ cups (300 mL) kirsch
⅓ cup (75 mL) sugar

DOUGH
1 oz (30 g) fresh yeast
2 cups (500 mL) lukewarm milk
2 cups (500 mL) flour
¼ cup (50 mL) granulated sugar
Pinch of salt
¼ cup (50 mL) softened butter
Simple syrup for brushing (see p. 152)

Preheat the oven to 375°F (190°C).

Soak the pears, apples, and prunes in hot water for 3 hours. Mix with the raisins, currants, and mixed peel. Chop the fruit. Stir in the walnuts, almonds, cinnamon, and star anise. Soak overnight in the kirsch and the sugar.

Meanwhile, make a levain (bread starter) by mixing the yeast, ¼ cup (50 mL) of the lukewarm milk, and 3 tbsp (45 mL) of the flour, or enough to bind the milk and yeast. Cover the ball with a cloth and put it in the warmest room in your house until it doubles in volume, about 1 to 1½ hours.

In a stand mixer with the hook attachment, mix the remaining flour, sugar, salt, and the remaining lukewarm milk. Add the levain and the butter and knead until the dough no longer sticks to the bowl. If the dough is not firm enough, add more flour.

Set the bowl aside, cover with a cloth, and place in the warmest room of the house. Let rise for 1 to 1½ hours. When the dough has risen, add the macerated fruit and mix well.

On a flour-dusted work surface, divide the dough and roll into 3 small loaves. Brush the loaves with simple syrup. Return to the warm room for at least 2 hours.

Bake for 45 minutes to 1 hour, or until a knife inserted in the middle of the loaf comes out clean. Wrap in plastic wrap and keep in your pantry for 3 to 4 weeks before Christmas. Cut into slices and serve with rumtopf (see p. 159).

This ancient method of cooking can be applied to everything from fish and chicken to root vegetables. It turns foie gras into a conversation piece. The salt seals the liver, keeping its moisture inside. And when it's cracked at the table, it reveals a showstopper.

SERVES 4

6 lb (3 kg) coarse sea salt
6 tbsp (90 mL) flour
3 egg whites
1 bunch thyme, chopped
½ tsp (2 mL) Szechuan peppercorns
½ tsp (2 mL) ground cinnamon
½ tsp (2 mL) ground star anise

¼ tsp (1 mL) ground cloves
1 duck foie gras loaf, approx. 14–18 oz (400–500 g)
¾ cup (175 mL) duck jus (see p. 219)
1½ tsp (7 mL) Vin Jaune (aged white wine) vinegar
1 tbsp (15 mL) butter
Salt and pepper to taste

Preheat the oven to 400°F (200°C).

In a mixing bowl, combine the sea salt, flour, egg whites, thyme, peppercorns, cinnamon, star anise, and cloves. Pour a third of the mixture into an oven-safe dish. Lay the foie gras on top, then cover with the remaining mixture. Using your hands, mould the salt crust on top and around the foie gras, making sure it is entirely covered. Bake for 25 minutes.

Meanwhile, in a saucepan, reduce the duck stock by one-quarter. Add the vinegar and bring to a simmer. Whisk in the butter. Season to taste and set aside.

Remove the foie gras from the oven and carefully break and remove the salt crust without poking the foie gras. Place the foie gras on a cutting board. Slice it evenly and delicately place in the middle of a serving tray. Drizzle with the duck sauce and serve.

NOTE   Traditionally, in France, boudin blanc aux truffes (with truffles) is served around Christmastime. Every year I make it to remind me of home and serve it with my foie gras en croûte. To cook, place the boudin blanc aux truffes in a frying pan with a little grapeseed oil. Bake in a 300°F (150°C) oven until the casing colour changes to amber. Arrange on a platter with the foie gras.

Christmas season to me is measured in sleepless nights, endless batches of stollen, hundreds of hours spent by the baker's oven, and the hustle and bustle that never seems to end. But the moment the city quiets and Christmas Eve is finally upon us, it's my family that makes the gruelling month of December worthwhile. I dedicate this recipe to the coolest children on the planet: Jane, Robbi Jay, Jules, Emilia, and Eva.

SERVES 6 TO 8

9 small rennet apples
2 shallots, finely chopped
1½ tsp (7 mL) grapeseed oil
10 oz (300 g) pork sausage meat (mild, not spicy)
10 oz (300 g) chestnuts, blanched and peeled
1 egg white

1 whole goose, dressed
Sea salt and pepper to taste
½ cup (125 mL) softened butter
9 fresh figs
⅔ cup (150 mL) unsweetened chestnut purée
⅓ cup (75 mL) sugar

Preheat the oven to 350°F (180°C).

Peel and core one of the apples; slice in small pieces. In a sauté pan over medium heat, sauté the shallots and apple pieces in the grapeseed oil. Remove from the heat and let cool. Chill in the refrigerator for 1 hour.

In a stand mixer with the paddle attachment, mix together the sautéed shallots and apple, sausage, chestnuts, and egg white until well blended. The mixture should become glutinous.

Season the cavity of the goose with sea salt and pepper. With a large spoon, fill the cavity with the stuffing. Sew it closed. Massage the bird with ¼ cup (50 mL) of the butter and season with sea salt and pepper.

Transfer the bird to a roasting tray and place in the preheated oven. After 30 minutes, baste the goose and repeat every 15 minutes. Meanwhile, core the 8 remaining apples and slice them in the centre horizontally to make circles. Add the apples and figs to the roasting tray 1 hour into the cooking time. Test the goose for doneness after about 1½ hours—a meat thermometer should reach 160°F (70°C).

While the goose is roasting, mix the chestnut purée with the remaining softened butter and sugar in a mixing bowl. Set aside.

Once the goose is cooked, remove from the oven and set it on a cutting board. Cover with foil. Carefully remove the roasted apples and figs and set aside on a tray.

After the goose has rested for 20 minutes, carve the bird, arranging the meat in the middle of a serving platter. Surround the meat with the stuffing, then with the roasted apples and figs. Before serving, fill the apples with the chestnut purée.

Chestnut purée can be purchased at most large food markets.

SERVES 6

16 oz (450 g) mixed dried fruit (sultanas, raisins, currants)

1 oz (30 g) mixed candied peel, finely chopped

2 small apples, peeled, cored, and grated

Zest and juice of 1 orange

Zest and juice of 1 lemon

⅓ cup (75 mL) brandy

¼ cup (50 mL) self-rising flour, sifted

2 tsp (10 mL) cinnamon

½ tsp each ground nutmeg, allspice, and cloves

½ cup (250 mL) shredded suet

¾ cup (175 mL) granulated sugar

½ cup (250 mL) fresh bread crumbs

2 tbsp (30 mL) roughly chopped almonds

2 large eggs (preferably free-range)

Place the dried fruit, candied peel, apples, and orange and lemon juice in a large mixing bowl. Stir in the brandy. Cover and leave overnight on the countertop.

In a very large mixing bowl, combine the flour, cinnamon, and mixed spice. Add the suet, sugar, lemon and orange zest, bread crumbs, and almonds, and mix well. Fold in the marinated fruit. Beat the eggs lightly and stir into the batter. The mixture should have a soft consistency.

Lightly grease 2 pudding basins and spoon the mixture in, gently pressing down with the back of a spoon. Cover with a double layer of parchment paper, then a layer of foil. Tie down securely with string.

Place the puddings in a steaming basket and over a pot of boiling water. Steam, covered, for 6 to 7 hours, checking the water frequently to make sure it doesn't boil dry. Remove the pudding and cool completely. Take off the parchment paper and foil. Prick the pudding with a skewer and drizzle with a little extra brandy.

Cover with fresh parchment paper and re-tie with string. Store in cool, dark place until Christmas Day.

On Christmas Day, reheat the pudding by steaming it again for 1½ to 2 hours. Flambé with 2 tbsp (30 mL) of brandy and serve.

NOTE   To make self-rising flour, sift together 1 cup (250 mL) all-purpose flour, 1½ tsp (7 mL) baking powder, and ½ tsp (2 mL) salt.

Most of the sauces called for in the preceding recipes are included with them. This section covers the small handful that are not, as well as those that are used again and again—none more so than chicken stock, probably the most fundamental and essential basic of the French pantry. Without exaggeration, it's as indispensable as butter, salt, and pepper. The only difference is that you can make this one. And when you do, and make it right, it will add as much to the dish you build with it as does beurre Échirée on your bread compared with cheap salted butter, or fleur de sel and grains of paradise on your steak compared with table salt and pre-ground black pepper.

There are a few easy rules to remember when you prepare the stocks, sauces, and jus in this section and elsewhere. First, whenever wine is deployed in making a stock or a sauce it must be boiled to force out the alcohol, which left in place will ruin the flavour. Second, a stock must never be salted, primarily because this would render any reduction made with it inedible. Salt the finished product, not the components. Finally, when water is called for, please understand that it must be cold, because its relatively high oxygenation improves taste, and, most important, because only cold water will drive to the surface the impurities that must be skimmed when bones are boiled. Everything else herein is self-explanatory.

2 shallots, finely chopped
½ cup (125 mL) white wine
¼ cup (50 mL) white wine vinegar
¼ cup (50 mL) butter
¼ cup (50 mL) cream
Salt and pepper to taste

Sauté the shallots until slightly brown. Add the white wine and vinegar; bring to a boil over medium heat. Lower the heat, simmer, and reduce by one-quarter. Slowly stir in the butter, alternately removing the pan from the heat and returning it to low heat, while ensuring that the pan remains cool enough on the bottom to touch. Once all the butter has melted, pour in the cream and season to taste. Keep warm in a double boiler until ready to use.

1 leek (white part only), finely chopped
1 celery stalk, finely chopped
3½ oz (100 g) mushrooms
2 garlic cloves, crushed
¼ cup (50 mL) butter
4 lb (2 kg) chicken bones, rinsed
1¼ cups (300 mL) dry white wine
12 cups (3 L) cold water
2 sprigs parsley
2 sprigs thyme
2 bay leaves
¼ cup (50 mL) white peppercorns

In a large saucepan, briefly sweat the leek, celery, mushrooms, and garlic in the butter without colouring. Add the bones and the white wine and reduce by two-thirds. Cover the bones with water and bring to a boil over medium heat. Skim the impurities from the top. Throw in the parsley, thyme, bay leaves, and peppercorns. Lower the heat and simmer until reduced by half. Strain through a fine sieve.

1 leek (white part only), finely chopped
1 celery stalk, finely chopped
1 cup (250 mL) mushrooms
2 garlic cloves, crushed
¼ cup (50 mL) butter
4 lb (2 kg) chicken bones, rinsed

1¾ cups (425 mL) dry white wine
12 cups (3 L) water
2 sprigs of parsley
2 sprigs of thyme
2 bay leaves
¼ cup (50 mL) white peppercorns

Preheat oven to 375°F (190°C). Rinse the chicken bones and pat dry with paper towels. Roast until well browned, about 20 minutes. Transfer bones to a platter. Pour off fat. Deglaze pan with ½ cup (125 mL) white wine. Reserve.

In a large saucepan, briefly sweat the leek, celery, mushrooms, and garlic in the butter without colouring. Add the chicken bones and the white wine and reduce by two-thirds. Cover the bones with water and bring to a boil over medium heat. Skim the impurities from the top. Throw in the parsley, thyme, bay leaves, and peppercorns. Reduce the heat and simmer until reduced by half. Strain through a fine sieve and set aside to cool.

2 lb (1 kg) fish bones
1 small onion, finely diced
1 leek, finely diced
½ celery stalk, finely diced
3½ oz (100 g) white button mushrooms
¼ cup (50 mL) butter
1¼ cups (300 mL) dry white wine
6 cups (1.5 L) cold water
¼ cup (50 mL) white peppercorns
Fresh basil

To prepare the fish bones, cut the gills with scissors and roughly chop the bones. Soak in cold water for 5 minutes. Drain and set aside.

In a large saucepan, sweat the onion, leek, celery, and mushrooms with the butter for 2 to 3 minutes without colouring. Add the fish bones and the white wine, bringing to a simmer to cook off the alcohol. Pour in the water and bring to a boil. Boil for no longer than 2 minutes, then skim the impurities from the top using a slotted spoon. Reduce the heat and stir in the white peppercorns and basil. Simmer gently for 25 minutes. Strain the stock through a fine sieve and set aside to cool.

STAGE 1
9 lb (4 kg) lamb bones
¼ cup (50 mL) butter
1¼ cups (300 mL) diced onions
¾ cup (175 mL) diced carrots
1 garlic clove, halved, roots and
    extra peel removed
½ cup (125 mL) chopped fresh
    tomatoes
2 sprigs thyme
3 sprigs rosemary
3 gallons (12 L) water

STAGE 2
4 lb (2 kg) lamb bones
4 tsp (20 mL) butter
3 tbsp (45 mL) diced onions
¼ cup (50 mL) diced carrots
½ garlic clove, crushed
¼ cup (50 mL) chopped fresh
    tomatoes
2 sprigs rosemary
1 sprig thyme

Preheat the oven to 375°F (190°C).

STAGE 1
Roast the bones in a large roasting pan in the oven until brown. Remove the bones and place them in a stockpot. Skim the fat from the roasting pan and deglaze with 4 cups (1 L) of the water, scraping the bottom of the pan with a wooden spoon to loosen the caramelized juices. Pour the water and juices from the roasting pan into the stockpot.

Melt the butter in a saucepan and sweat the onions and carrots. Add the garlic and colour lightly. Mix in the fresh tomatoes and continue cooking until the vegetables are a rich brown. Pour in 4 cups (1 L) of the water and reduce by half; add to the stockpot. Add the remaining water, rosemary, and thyme. Bring to a brisk boil over high heat and skim the impurities. Lower the heat and simmer until reduced by half. Strain through a fine sieve.

STAGE 2
Repeat the steps in stage 1, roasting the bones and deglazing the pan; sweating the onions, carrots, garlic, and tomatoes; combining with the bones in the stockpot. Instead of water, add the stage 1 lamb jus, topping up with water if necessary and the rosemary and thyme. Bring to a brisk boil, simmer, and reduce by half. Strain through a fine sieve.

1 leek (white part only), finely chopped
1 celery stalk, finely chopped
1 cup (250 mL) mushrooms
2 garlic cloves, crushed
¼ cup (50 mL) butter
4 lb (2 kg) duck bones

12 cups (3 L) water
1¼ cups (300 mL) dry white wine
2 sprigs of parsley
2 sprigs of thyme
2 bay leaves
¼ cup (50 mL) white peppercorns

In a large saucepan, briefly sweat the leek, celery, mushrooms, and garlic in the butter without colouring. Add the duck bones and the white wine and reduce by two-thirds. Cover the bones with water and bring to a boil over medium heat. Skim the impurities from the top. Throw in the parsley, thyme, bay leaves, and peppercorns. Reduce the heat and simmer until reduced by half. Strain through a fine sieve and set aside to cool.

Bodies and shells from 4 lobsters
2 tbsp (30 mL) grapeseed oil
1 medium onion, chopped
1 celery stalk, chopped
1 carrot, chopped
2 garlic cloves, chopped
½ fennel, sliced
4 plum tomatoes, chopped
1 bay leaf
½ bunch tarragon
½ cup (125 mL) cognac
1 cup (250 mL) white wine
16 cups (4 L) water
Salt and pepper to taste

Break the lobster shells into small pieces. Open the bodies and remove the grey, feathery gills. Remove the sand sac from between the eyes. Crush the bodies so they will fit into a large stockpot.

Heat the grapeseed oil in the stockpot over medium heat and roast the lobster for 10 minutes or until golden brown. Add the onion, celery, and carrot and sauté for 3 to 4 minutes. Mix in the garlic and fennel and cook for another 2 to 3 minutes. Add the tomatoes, bay leaf, and tarragon. Deglaze with cognac and flambé. Stir in the white wine and the water, mixing well and cooking until the alcohol largely burns off the wine, about 3 to 4 minutes.

Bring to a boil, then turn down to a simmer. Simmer gently for at least 90 minutes. Season with salt and pepper to taste. When the stock tastes full-flavoured, strain by turning off the heat, then grabbing all the big chunks with tongs and tossing them in the trash. Strain the remaining liquid through a fine-mesh sieve with a piece of cheesecloth set inside it.

4 lb (2 kg) vine-ripened red tomatoes (about 10 medium)
6 basil leaves
4 tsp (20 mL) sea salt

Rinse the tomatoes well under running water and slice them into quarters. In a food processor, purée the tomatoes, basil, and salt until smooth. Line a large sieve with cheesecloth and place over a tall metal bowl. Carefully pour the purée into the centre of the cheesecloth. Transfer the sieve and bowl to the fridge and allow the tomatoes to strain overnight. Retain the liquid that has collected in the bowl.

Veal Jus

MAKES APPROX. 12 CUPS (3 L)

STAGE 1

13 lb (6 kg) veal bones (neck and back)

4 cups (1 L) rich red wine

2½ cups (625 mL) celery, cut in 1½-inch (4 cm) strips

1½ cups (375 mL) carrots, cut in 1½-inch (4 cm) strips (mirepoix)

½ cup (125 mL) onions, cut in 1½-inch (4 cm) strips

2 garlic cloves, halved, root and excess skin removed

3 tbsp (45 mL) grapeseed oil

¾ cup (175 mL) tomato paste

1¼ cups (300 mL) port

2½ gallons (10 L) water

4 sprigs thyme

5 bay leaves

¼ cup (50 mL) crushed peppercorns

STAGE 2

6 lb (3 kg) veal bones (neck and back)

2 cups (500 mL) red wine

1 cup (250 mL) chopped leeks (white part only)

¾ cup (175 mL) carrots, cut in 1½-inch (4 cm) strips

¼ cup (50 mL) chopped onions

1 garlic clove, halved, root and excess skin removed

3 tbsp (45 mL) tomato paste

Preheat the oven to 375°F (190°C).

STAGE 1

Rinse the bones in cold water and pat dry. Place in a roasting pan and roast in the oven until golden brown. Remove the bones and transfer to a stockpot. Pour off the fat and then deglaze the pan with 2 cups (500 mL) of the red wine, scraping the bottom of the pan with a wooden spoon to capture the caramelized juices. Add the wine and juices from the pan to the stockpot.

In a large, heavy-bottomed saucepan, sweat the celery, carrots, onions, and garlic in grapeseed oil until lightly coloured. Add the tomato paste and port and stir continuously, taking care not to burn the tomato or the vegetables. When nicely browned, deglaze with the remaining 2 cups (500 mL) red wine, stirring and scraping the bottom of the pan to loosen the caramelized parts and capture the flavour. Reduce by half and add to the bones and wine in the stockpot. Pour in the water, place on high heat, and bring to a brisk boil, skimming the impurities from the surface. Add the thyme, bay leaves, and crushed peppercorns and simmer until reduced by a third.

Strain through a muslin cloth. Discard the bones and set aside.

STAGE 2

Repeat the steps in stage 1: roast the bones and deglaze the pan with 1 cup (250 mL) of the red wine. Sweat the leeks, carrots, onions, and garlic in a saucepan. Mix with the tomato paste and deglaze with the remaining red wine, reducing by half. Add to the bones and wine in the stockpot.

This time, add the stage 1 veal jus to the stockpot, topping up with cold water if necessary. Bring to a brisk boil over high heat, skimming the impurities from the surface. Strain the remaining liquid through a muslin cloth and discard the bones.

Court Bouillon

MAKES APPROX. 4 CUPS (1 L)

2 leek leaves
3 sprigs thyme
3 sprigs parsley
3 bay leaves (preferably fresh)
1 carrot, peeled and chopped
1 onion, peeled and chopped
1 tbsp (15 mL) grey sea salt
8 black peppercorns
4 cups (1 L) water
½ cup (125 mL) white wine vinegar

Tie the leek leaves, thyme, parsley, and bay leaves together to make a bouquet garni. Add the bouquet, carrot, onion, sea salt, peppercorns, water, and vinegar to a saucepan, bringing to a boil over high heat. Lower the heat and simmer for 8 to 10 minutes. Remove from heat and strain through a muslin cloth. Always bring to a boil before using.

Coriander Aïoli

MAKES APPROX. ½ CUP (125 mL)

2 garlic cloves
1 large egg yolk
2 tsp (10 mL) fresh lemon juice
½ tsp (5 mL) Dijon mustard
¼ cup (50 mL) extra-virgin olive oil
3 tbsp (45 mL) vegetable oil
2 tbsp (30 mL) chopped fresh coriander
Salt and pepper to taste

Mince and mash the garlic to a paste with a pinch of salt, using a large, heavy knife. Whisk together the egg yolk, lemon juice, and mustard in a bowl. In a separate bowl, combine the olive oil and vegetable oil. Add the oils a few drops at a time to the yolk mixture, whisking continuously until all the oil is incorporated and the mixture is emulsified and thick. Whisk in the garlic paste and coriander; season with salt and pepper. If the aïoli looks too thick, whisk in 1 or 2 drops of water. Cover and chill until ready to use.

NOTE If the mixture separates, stop adding the oil and continue whisking until it comes together again, then resume.

Avocado Mayonnaise

2 egg yolks
2 tbsp (30 mL) white wine vinegar
1 tbsp (15 mL) Dijon mustard
1 avocado, peeled, stoned, and mashed
2 cups (500 mL) avocado oil
Juice of ½ a lemon
Salt and pepper to taste

Combine the egg yolks, vinegar, mustard, and avocado in a food processor, blending for 1 to 2 minutes. With the machine running, slowly pour in the avocado oil and lemon juice; blend until thick. Season to taste and refrigerate.

Green Oil

1 cup fresh basil leaves, blanched
1½ cups (375 mL) extra-virgin olive oil

Purée the basil and olive oil in a blender until smooth.

Citrus Vinaigrette

Juice of 2 limes
Juice of 2 lemons
Juice of 1 orange
2 tbsp (30 mL) sherry vinegar
½ cup (125 mL) extra-virgin olive oil
1 tbsp (15 mL) maple syrup
Pinch of salt

Combine the lime, lemon, and orange juice and the vinegar in a bowl. Whisk in the olive oil and maple syrup. Add salt to taste. Pour in a clear, tall container and refrigerate.

White Truffle Vinaigrette

4 tsp (20 mL) fresh lemon juice
Salt and pepper to taste
4 tbsp (60 mL) white truffle oil
1 tsp (5 mL) chopped white truffle

Whisk the lemon juice and salt and pepper in a mixing bowl. Slowly add the white truffle oil while continuing to whisk. Stir in the chopped white truffles.

Citrus Coulis

2 cups (500 mL) water
1½ cups (375 mL) sugar
Juice of 2 oranges
1 orange
1 tbsp (15 mL) chopped ginger

Make a simple syrup by boiling the water with the sugar to create a clear syrup. Combine 2 cups (500 mL) of the syrup with the orange juice in a small saucepan and warm over medium heat. Peel and chop the whole orange (removing all pith) and add to the mixture with the ginger. Cook until the mixture is reduced by half. Set aside to cool.

Mango Coulis

1 mango, peeled
¾ to 1 cup (175 to 250 mL) maple syrup
2 passion fruits

Thinly slice the mango and finely chop. Warm a small saucepan over medium heat and add the mango and maple syrup, adjusting the amount depending on the sweetness of the fruit. Slice the passion fruit in half lengthwise and scoop out the insides into the pan; mix to combine. Bring to a boil and reduce, stirring occasionally, for 5 minutes until thick and syrupy.

ACKNOWLEDGMENTS

Nothing is more special than a table surrounded by friends and family. Even the finest feast can't compare.

In my life, it's always been the women who ruled the homestead. And it's these inspiring women who raised me and taught me the value and enjoyment of hosting people in our home and the fine art of creating memorable meals. They were the ones who brought people together, whether for a special occasion or just because. Our table was always crowded and everybody was always welcome. I carry that with me today.

The meals were simple and well chosen, made from what was fresh and readily available. And more often than not, it was the actual cooking that brought us together—it was as social as the meal itself.

I'd like to thank my mother, Jeanne, my grandmothers, and all my aunts for these early, invaluable lessons. I feel fortunate to have inherited their shared love of food and eating.

At a young age, and in an earnest effort to keep out of trouble, I followed my cousins to the nearby kitchens of Chez Pierre and Boulangerie Thuet in Blodelsheim.

Here my two uncles, Pierre and Marcel, taught us the fundamentals of running a kitchen. They helped instill an early and lifelong passion for cooking, although their success wasn't as great in keeping me out of trouble. Not their fault. I can't thank them enough for the life lessons they contributed to my upbringing.

Later, I entered cooking school in Strasbourg and spent my weekends and hours after school in the kitchens of the great Antoine Westerman of Buerehiesel and Emile Yung of Au Crocodile. They showed me that dedication and hard work is the recipe for success. *Merci beaucoup.*

I'd also like to thank the late Roelly family. Chef Roelly was the one who taught me to hunt (and did his best to instill the rebel in me). *Merci, je pense.*

I owe a huge debt of gratitude to the great and talented Chef Anton Mosimann, whom I first worked with at the Dorchester in London. I'm happy to have this opportunity to thank him for his profound culinary enlightenment. To this day, and in these particularly tough times, his motto "happy chefs, happy cooking" rings true in my ear. And much respect to Ralph Burgin. He arrived in London from the famed kitchen of Eckart Witzigmann and was instrumental in the Dorchester's Le Terrace being named the top restaurant in the world, outside of France.

When I came to Canada, Chef Albert Schnell was my first link to the kitchens of this great country. He is undoubtedly one of the founders of Canadian cuisine as we know it today. I thank him for introducing me to the vast number of fine ingredients this country has to offer.

To my dear friend, the late Willy Fida, I thank you for spending your time with us back then and sharing your culinary education with all the chefs in the Châteauneuf brigade.

To my second family in Canada, Franco and Barbara Prevedello, I wouldn't be where I am today without all your love and support. Thank you.

I'd also like to express my appreciation and admiration for the countless suppliers, farmers, and colleagues who are always so gracious and supportive of my businesses (not to mention my nocturnal patterns and demands). I have such respect for their tireless efforts in providing me, and ultimately my customers, with the finest and freshest products on the market today. In particular, Beretta Organic Farms, the Butcher Shoppe, François Kovalski, the Herbman, Kobe Classic Beef, Donato Harvest, and especially Ray Hart from Sheridan Foods, who has never let me down over the past twenty years. It's an honour doing business with all of you.

I am deeply grateful to the talented team at Cineflix Productions, and give a special nod to Simon Lloyd, Karen Dougherty, and the genius and dedicated Jo Cross. A special nod also to the amazing Nick Cory-Wright, who is the official recipient of the lustrous award for perseverance/guardianship of my work. You forced me to make my deadlines and worked so long and hard to help me get this and other projects off the ground.

Thank you to my editorial team at Penguin, especially Andrea Magyar. Your patience with me is duly noted. And thanks to Mary Opper for her talent in designing the book.

Thank you to Paula Wilson. Your photographs beautifully capture the essence of my recipes. And your impressive ability to deal with my many moods definitely brought this book to life. Thank you for your patience and creative eye.

To Tim and Laura from Empire PR, for their many laughs and late-night brainstorming sessions around the dining-room table. (And thanks, Tim, for taking some of my incomprehensible thoughts and words and translating them into English!)

To the two great culinary gurus of Toronto, Jacob Richler and James Chatto, I thank you for not only following my career but, most importantly, sharing your enjoyment and love of food with me and all your readers. I respect you for challenging me all these years.

I firmly believe the measure of a chef is his kitchen brigade. From the bottom of my heart, I'd like to thank my extended family of chefs who, throughout the years, have tirelessly worked alongside me and courageously tolerated my many tempers (and perhaps the occasional tirade) in our quest for perfection.

In particular, special thanks to Jay Moore and Motonobu Nishimura. Your talent and professionalism are remarkable and allowed me to make this book a reality.

And to Martial for bringing your talent to my bakery and giving us our daily bread!

As I mentioned earlier, I entered this world surrounded by women, and the same holds true today. My family is my motivation and moral support for doing it all. I save my deepest gratitude for them. In addition to my mother, grandmothers, and aunts, I thank my father, Robert, who was taken too soon, but taught me at a young age the very definition of hard work. To my brothers, Serge and Michel, I'm grateful for your lifelong belief in and support for what I do.

To Dragan, thank you for helping me debone what must now be countless carcasses and for crafting with me the culinary world's first, one-of-a-kind Serb-Alsatian charcuterie.

To our Mira, the support you give to me and my family is amazing. And your first-class service of coffee and breakfast is my morning fuel.

To Bissa and Maya, I can't thank you enough for keeping my blonde ambition so alive (literally and figuratively).

To my dear daughters, Jane and Robbi Jay. Thank you for everything, not least for the countless days and nights you spent happily typing my recipes and learning about my life, at the expense of going out to enjoy your own.

To my son, Jules. I thank you for making me laugh and for not ignoring all those early-morning wake-up calls. As well, for your personal attention to the Petite Thuet stores during the making of this book.

To my darling littlest girls, Emilia and Eva. Thank you for being you and for giving up your living spaces so we could crowd around your pretty pink computer while we wrote and researched this book. You are the dearest gofers the world has ever known.

Without a doubt, I want to express my love and admiration to my better half, Bee. I am grateful for your daily contribution of time, love, and support. Just having you near makes me stronger. You are my pillar and my partner in business and in life, and you provide me with the hunger to cook and to create. Your faith makes life so easy for this chef. *Ton investissement quotidien et ta présence rassurante me donnent la force de me surpasser.*

And last but not least, to my readers and clients. Thank you. You allow me to be the person I was born and raised to be.

INDEX

Marc Thuet, a fourth-generation chef born in Alsace, France, is renowned for his culinary talents. Along with his wife and business partner, Biana Zorich, he owns businesses that include several Petite Thuet bakery cafés. The opening of their Conviction restaurant launched the popular reality TV food show *Conviction Kitchen* featuring the famous couple. Marc Thuet lives in Toronto with his family.